Harvard
Business
Review

ON
CULTURE AND CHANGE

THE HARVARD BUSINESS REVIEW PAPERBACK SERIES

The series is designed to bring today's managers and professionals the fundamental information they need to stay competitive in a fast-moving world. From the preeminent thinkers whose work has defined an entire field to the rising stars who will redefine the way we think about business, here are the leading minds and landmark ideas that have established the *Harvard Business Review* as required reading for ambitious businesspeople in organizations around the globe.

Other books in the series:

Other books in the series (continued):

Harvard Business Review

ON

CULTURE AND CHANGE

A HARVARD BUSINESS REVIEW PAPERBACK

The *Harvard Business Review* articles in this collection are available as
individual reprints. Discounts apply to quantity purchases. For information and ordering, please contact Customer Service, Harvard Business
School Publishing, Boston, MA 02163. Telephone: (617) 783-7500 or
(800) 988-0886, 8 A.M. to 6 P.M. Eastern Time, Monday through Friday.
Fax: (617) 783-7555, 24 hours a day. E-mail: custserv@hbsp.harvard.edu

978-1-57851-836-4 (ISBN 13)

Library of Congress Control Number: 2002100250

Contents

Harvard Business Review

ON

CULTURE AND CHANGE

The Nut Island Effect

When Good Teams Go Wrong

PAUL F. LEVY

Executive Summary

THE TEAM THAT OPERATED the Nut Island sewage treatment plant in Quincy, Massachusetts, was every manager's dream. Members of the group performed difficult, dangerous work without complaint. They needed little supervision. They improvised their way around operational difficulties and budgetary constraints. They were dedicated to the organization's mission.

But their hard work let to catastrophic failure. How could such a good team go so wrong? In this article, the author tells the story of the Nut Island plant and identifies a common, yet destructive organizational dynamic that can strike any business.

The Nut Island effect begins with a deeply committed team that is isolated from a company's mainstream activities. Pitted against this team is its senior management. Preoccupied with high-visibility problems, management assigns the team a vital but behind-the-scenes task. Allowed considerable autonomy, team members become adept at managing themselves. Management takes the team's self-sufficiency for granted and ignores team members when they ask for help. When trouble strikes and management is unresponsive, team members feel betrayed and develop an us-against-the-world mentality. They stay out of management's line of sight, hiding problems. The team begins to make up its own rules, which mask grave problems in its operations. Management, disinclined in the first place to focus on the team's work, is easily misled by team members' skillful disguising of its performance deficiencies. The resulting stalemate typically can be broken only by an external event.

The Nut Island story serves as a warning to managers who concentrate their efforts on their organization's most visible shortcomings: sometimes the most debilitating problems are the ones we can't see.

THEY WERE EVERY MANAGER'S dream team. They performed difficult, dirty, dangerous work without complaint, they put in thousands of hours of unpaid overtime, and they even dipped into their own pockets to buy spare parts. They needed virtually no supervision, handled their own staffing decisions, cross-trained each other, and ingeniously improvised their way around operational difficulties and budgetary constraints. They had tremendous esprit de corps and a deep commitment to the organization's mission.

There was just one problem: their hard work helped lead to that mission's catastrophic failure.

The team that traced this arc of futility were the 80 or
so men and women who operated the Nut Island sewage
treatment plant in Quincy, Massachusetts, from the late
1960s until it was decommissioned in 1997. During that
period, these exemplary workers were determined to
protect Boston Harbor from pollution. Yet in one six-
month period in 1982, in the ordinary course of business,
they released 3.7 billion gallons of raw sewage into the
harbor. Other routine procedures they performed to keep
the harbor clean, such as dumping massive amounts of
chlorine into otherwise untreated sewage, actually wors-
ened the harbor's already dreadful water quality.

How could such a good team go so wrong? And why
were the people of the Nut Island plant—not to mention
their supervisors in Boston—unable to recognize that
they were sabotaging themselves and their mission?
These questions go to the heart of what I call *the Nut
Island effect*, a destructive organizational dynamic I
came to understand after serving four and a half years as
the executive director of the public authority responsible
for the metropolitan Boston sewer system.

Since leaving that job, I have shared the Nut Island
story with managers from a wide range of organizations.
Quite a few of them—hospital administrators, research
librarians, senior corporate officers—react with a shock
of recognition. They, too, have seen the Nut Island effect
in action where they work.

Comparing notes with these managers, I have found
that each instance of the Nut Island effect features a similar set of antagonists—a dedicated, cohesive team and
distracted senior managers—whose conflict follows a
predictable behavioral pattern through five stages. (The
path of the Nut Island effect is illustrated in "Five Steps to

Failure" at the end of this article.) The sequence of the stages may vary somewhat from case to case, but in its broad outlines, the syndrome is unchanging. In a dynamic that is not so much a vicious circle as a vicious spiral, the relationship between the two sides gradually crumbles under the weight of mutual mistrust and incomprehension until it can hardly be called a relationship at all.

The consequences of this organizational pathology are not always as vivid and unmistakable as they were in the case of the Nut Island team. More frequently, I suspect, its effects are like a slow leak—subtle, gradual, and difficult to trace. Nevertheless, the Nut Island story should serve as a warning to managers who spend the bulk of their time on an organization's most visible and obvious shortcomings: sometimes the most debilitating problems are the ones we can't see.

The Nut Island Effect Defined

The Nut Island effect begins with a homogeneous, deeply committed team working in isolation that can be physical, psychological, or both. Pitted against this team are its senior supervisors, who are usually separated from the team by several layers of management. In the first stage of the Nut Island effect, senior management, preoccupied with high-visibility problems, assigns the team a vital but behind-the-scenes task. This is a crucial feature: the team carries out its task far from the eye of the public or customers. Allowed a great deal of autonomy, team members become adept at organizing and managing themselves, and the unit develops a proud and distinct identity. In the second stage, senior management begins to take the team's self-sufficiency for granted and ignores team members when they ask for help or try to warn of impending trouble. Management's apparent indifference breeds resentment in the team members, reinforces its isolation, and heightens its sense of itself as a band of heroic outcasts. In the third stage, an us-against-the-world mentality takes hold among team members. They make it a priority to stay out of management's line of sight, which leads them to deny or minimize problems and avoid asking for help.

This isolation leads to the fourth stage of the conflict. With no external input on practices and operating guidelines, the team begins to make up its own rules. The team tells itself that the rules enable it to fulfill its mission. In fact, these rules mask the deterioration of the team's working environment and deficiencies in the team's performance. In the fifth stage, both the team and senior management form distorted pictures of reality that are very difficult to correct. Team members come to believe they are the only ones who really understand their work. They close their ears when well-meaning outsiders attempt to point out problems. Management tells itself that no news is good news and continues to ignore the team and its task. Only some kind of external event can break this stalemate. Perhaps management disbands the team or pulls the plug on its project. Perhaps a crisis forces the team to ask for help and snaps management out of its complacency. Even then, team members may not understand the extent of their difficulties or recognize that their efforts may have aggravated the very problems they were attempting to solve. Management, for its part, may be unable to recognize the role it played in setting in motion this self-reinforcing spiral of failure.

That, then, is an outline of the Nut Island effect. Here is how it played out at a small sewage treatment plant on the edge of Boston Harbor.

The Nut Island Story

Nut Island is actually a small peninsula in Quincy, Massachusetts, a mostly blue-collar city of 85,000 located about ten miles south of Boston. Sitting at the southern entrance to Boston Harbor, Nut Island was a favorite landmark for seventeenth-century sailors, who savored the scent of what one early European settler called the "divers arematicall herbes, and plants" that grew there. "Shipps have come from Virginea where there have bin scarce five men able to hale a rope," the settler wrote, "untill they come [near Nut Island], and smell the sweet aire of the shore, where they have suddainly recovered."

By 1952, when the Nut Island treatment plant went into operation, the herbs and sweet air were long gone. Before the plant came on line, raw sewage from much of Boston and the surrounding area was piped straight into the harbor, fouling local beaches and fisheries and posing a serious health hazard to the surrounding community.

The Nut Island plant was billed as the solution to Quincy's wastewater problem. Hailed in the local press for its "modern design," it was supposed to treat all the sewage produced in the southern half of the Boston metropolitan area, then release it about a mile out into the harbor. From the first, though, the plant's suitability for the task was questionable. The facility was designed to handle sewage inflows of up to 285 million gallons per day, comfortably above the 112 million gallons that flowed in on an average day. But high tides and heavy rains could increase the flow to three times the daily average, straining the plant to its limits and compromising its performance.

During most of the 30 years covered in this article, the team charged with running the plant was headed by superintendent Bill Smith, operations chief Jack Madden, and laboratory head Frank Mac Kinnon. The three joined me recently for a reunion at Nut Island, which has been converted to a headworks that collects sewage from the southern Boston region and delivers it north through a tunnel under Boston Harbor to the city's vast new treatment plant on Deer Island. The men's affection for each other is evident, as are the lingering remnants of plant hierarchy. When someone has to speak for the entire group, Mac Kinnon and Madden still defer to Smith.

The three friends don't need much prompting to launch into reminiscences of their years at Nut Island, which they still view as the happiest time of their working lives. They laugh often as they tell stories about the old days, featuring characters with nicknames like Sludgie and Twinkie, and they seem cheerfully oblivious to the hair-raising conditions that were part of daily life at the plant. When Smith talks about once finding himself neck-deep in wastewater as he worked in the pump room, he speaks without a hint of horror or disgust. It's just a good story. "It was fun," Smith says, and his two friends nod in agreement. Holding an old sewer plant together with chewing gum and baling wire really is their idea of a good time.

Throughout our talk, the men frequently refer to themselves and their coworkers as a family. But Nut Island had not always been such a harmonious place. When Smith arrived there in 1963, fresh out of the navy, he walked into a three-way cold war among operations, maintenance, and the plant's laboratory. Each side viewed its own function as essential and looked down on the other groups' workers as incompetents. "The maintenance guys thought the lab guys were a bunch of college boys," says Smith, a short, powerfully built man who at age 63 still has more black than gray in his long, pony-tailed hair and thick beard. "And the guys in the lab said the maintenance guys were just grease monkeys."

For the next few years, Smith did what he could to "get a little cooperation going." By 1968, he had gained Madden and Mac Kinnon as allies. Before long, they had weeded out most of the plant's shirkers and complainers and assembled a cohesive team. The people they hired were much like themselves: hardworking, grateful for the security of a public sector job, and happy to stay out of the spotlight. Many were veterans of World War II or the Korean War, accustomed to managing frequent crises in harsh working conditions—just what awaited them at the aging, undersized, underfunded plant. Tony Kucikas was typical of the breed. He signed on in 1968 after being discharged from the navy, where he had worked as an engineer and machinist. When he walked into the plant on his first day, even the smell of oil was familiar, he recalls. "It reminded me so much of the engine room," he says, smiling at the memory. "I can remember walking down those first stairs and saying to myself, 'I'm going to like this,' because I felt right at home."

Nut Island's hiring practices helped create a tight-knit group, bonded by a common cause and shared values, but they also eliminated any "squeaky wheels" who might have questioned the team's standard operating procedures or alerted senior management to the plant's deteriorating condition. That was fine with Smith and his colleagues. Assembling a like-minded group made it easier for them to break down interdepartmental ani-mosities by cross-training plant personnel. The team leaders also made job satisfaction a priority, shifting peo-ple out of the jobs they were hired to do and into work that suited them better. These moves raised morale and created a strong sense of trust and ownership among plant workers.

Just how strong the sense of ownership was can be seen in the sacrifices the team made. Few people on Nut Island made more than $20,000 a year, low wages even in the 1960s and 1970s. Yet when there was no money for spare parts, team members would pitch in to buy the needed equipment. They were equally generous with their time. A sizable cadre of plant workers regularly put in far more than the requisite eight hours daily, but they only occasionally filed for overtime pay. In fact, several of the Nut Island alumni I interviewed seemed almost embarrassed when the subject came up, as if there was something slightly shameful about claiming the extra time.

From 1952 until 1985, the Nut Island plant fell under the purview of the Metropolitan District Commission (MDC), a regional infrastructure agency responsible for Greater Boston's parks and recreation areas, some of its major roads, and its water supplies and sewers. (In 1985, the Massachusetts state legislature, under pressure from a federal lawsuit, shifted responsibility for water and sewers to a new entity, the Massachusetts Water Resources Authority.) Throughout the early and mid-1900s, the MDC had been known for the quality of its engineers and the rigor of its management. It had constructed and operated water and sewer systems that were often cited as engineering marvels. By the 1960s, though, the MDC had become the plaything of the state legislature, whose members used the agency as a patronage mill. Commissioners rarely stayed more than two years, and their priorities reflected those of the legislators who controlled the MDC budget. The lawmakers understood full well that there were more votes to be gained by building skating rinks and swimming pools in their districts than by tuning up the sewer system, and they directed their funding and political pressure accordingly. As a result, control of Greater Boston's sewer system fell into the hands of political functionaries whose primary concern was to please their patrons in the statehouse. If that meant building another skating rink instead of maintaining Nut Island, so be it.

The attitude of the MDC's leadership toward the sewer division can be gauged by a story that became a staple of plant lore. As it was passed around, the story took on mythic power. It became a central component of the Nut Island team's self-definition.

It seems that one day, James W. Connell, Nut Island superintendent in the 1960s, went to Boston to ask the MDC commissioner for funds to perform long-deferred maintenance on essential equipment. The commissioner's only response: "Get rid of the dandelions."

Startled, the superintendent asked the commissioner to repeat himself.

"You heard me. I want you guys to take some money and get the dandelions off the lawn. The place looks terrible."

The story speaks for itself, but I would point out that it was something of a miracle that the commissioner had even laid eyes on the lawn and its dandelions. Visits to Nut Island by the MDC's upper management were so rare that when one commissioner did show up at the plant, workers there failed to recognize him and ordered him off the premises. For the most part, Smith says, "We did our thing, and they just left us alone."

At this point, the first stage of the Nut Island effect is in place. We have a distracted management and a dedicated team that toils, by choice, in obscurity. They are

isolated not only from management but from their customers—in this case, the public. Team members, who
share a similar background, value system, and outlook,
have enormous trust in each other and very little in outsiders, especially management. Now, an egregious display of indifference from management is all it takes to
set the downward spiral in motion.

On Nut Island, this display came in January 1976,
when the plant's four gigantic diesel engines shut down.
The disaster was predictable. Since the early 1970s, the
workers at Nut Island had been warning the top brass in
Boston that the engines, which pumped wastewater into
the plant and then through a series of aeration and treatment tanks, desperately needed maintenance. The MDC,
though, had refused to release any funds to maintain
them. Make do with what you have, plant operators were
told. When something stops working, we'll find you the
money to fix it. In essence, the MDC's management
refused to act until a crisis forced their hand. That crisis
arrived when the engines gave out entirely. The team at
the plant worked frantically to get the engines running
again, but for four days, untreated sewage flowed into
the harbor.

The incident propelled the conflict between the Nut
Island team and senior management from the second
stage to the third—from passive resentment to active
avoidance. The plant workers viewed the breakdown as a
mortifying failure that they could have averted if MDC
headquarters had listened to them instead of cutting
them adrift. In ordinary circumstances, management's
indifference might have killed off the team's morale
and motivation. It had the opposite effect on the Nut
Islanders. They united around a common adversary. Nut
Island was *their* plant, and its continued operation was

solely the result of their own heroic efforts. No bureau-
crat in Boston was going to stop them from running it
the way it ought to be run. (To this day, the workers at
Nut Island deny that their cohesiveness stemmed from
their shared disdain for headquarters; "I don't want to
give them credit for *anything*," one worker told me
recently.)

It became a priority among the Nut Islanders to avoid
contact with upper management whenever possible.
When the plant ran short of ferrous chloride, a chemical
used for odor control, no
one from Nut Island
asked headquarters for
funds to buy a new sup-
ply. Instead, they would
contact a local commu-
nity activist and ask her
to complain to her state representative about odors ema-
nating from the plant. The rep would then contact MDC
headquarters, and Nut Island would receive a fresh supply of ferrous chloride. In part, this was a case of shrewd
"managing upward" by Bill Smith and his colleagues. But
it also shows how far the team would go to avoid dealing
with management.

*Isolated in its lonely outpost,
its stock of ideas limited
to those of its own members,
the team begins to
make up its own rules.*

Another way the Nut Islanders stayed off management's radar screen was to keep their machinery running
long past the time it should have been overhauled or
junked. Their repairs often showed great ingenuity—at
times they even manufactured their own parts on-site.
Ultimately, though, the team's resourcefulness compromised the very job they were supposed to accomplish.

Among the plant's most troublesome equipment were
the pumps that drew sludge—fecal matter and other
solids—into the digester tanks. Inside the tanks, anaero-
bic bacteria were added to eliminate the pathogens in

the sludge, reduce its volume, and render it safe for release into the harbor. Years of deferred maintenance had degraded the pumps, but instead of asking Boston for funds to replace them, the Nut Islanders lubricated the machinery with lavish amounts of oil. Much of this oil found its way into the digester tanks themselves. From there, it was released into the harbor. (Beginning in 1991, treated sludge was shipped to a nearby facility for conversion to fertilizer.) A former sewer division scientist tells me he suspects the releases of tainted sludge account for the high concentration of oil in Boston Harbor's sediments, compared with other harbors on the East Coast.

Rules of Thumb

A team can easily lose sight of the big picture when it is narrowly focused on a demanding task. The task itself becomes the big picture, crowding other considerations out of the frame. To counteract this tendency, smart managers supply reality checks by exposing their people to the perspectives and practices of other organizations. (For other suggestions, see "How to Stop the Nut Island Effect Before It Starts" at the end of this article.) A team in the fourth stage of the Nut Island effect, however, is denied this exposure. Isolated in its lonely outpost, its stock of ideas limited to those of its own members, the team begins to make up its own rules. These rules are terribly insidious because they foster in the team and its management the mistaken belief that its operations are running smoothly.

On Nut Island, one such rule governed the amount of grit—the sand, dirt, and assorted particulate crud that inevitably finds its way into wastewater—that the plant workers considered acceptable. Because of a flaw in the plant's design, its aeration tanks would become choked with grit if the inflow of sewage exceeded a certain volume. The plant operators dealt with this problem by limiting inflows to what they considered a manageable level, diverting the excess into the harbor. Reflecting the distorted perspective typical of teams in the grip of the Nut Island effect, these diversions were not even recorded as overflows from the plant because the excess wastewater did not, strictly speaking, enter the facility.

Another rule of thumb governed the use of chlorine at Nut Island. When inflows were particularly heavy, even the sewage that flowed through the plant did not always undergo full treatment. The plant's operators would add massive amounts of chlorine to some of the wastewater and pipe it out to sea. The chlorine eliminated some pathogens in the wastewater, but its other effects were less benign. Classified by the Environmental Protection Agency as an environmental contaminant, chlorine kills marine life, depletes marine oxygen supplies, and harms fragile shore ecosystems. To the team on Nut Island, though, chlorine was better than nothing. By their reckoning, they were giving the wastewater at least minimal treatment—thus their indignant denials when Quincy residents complained of raw sewage in the water and on their beaches.

In its fifth stage, the Nut Island effect generates its own reality-distortion field. This process is fairly straightforward in management's case. Disinclined in the first place to look too closely at the team's operations, management is easily misled by the team's skillful disguising of its flaws and deficiencies. In fact, it wants to be misled—it has enough problems on its plate. One reason MDC management left Nut Island alone is that even as it was falling apart, the plant looked clean, especially compared to the old Deer Island plant, which suffered a very public series of breakdowns in the 1970s and 1980s. Reassured by Nut Island's patina of efficiency, the MDC's upper management focused on business that seemed more pressing.

The manner in which team members delude themselves is somewhat more complicated. Part of their self-deception involves wishful thinking—the common human tendency to reject information that clashes with the reality one wishes to see. Consider, for instance, the laboratory tests performed at the plant. These tests were required by the EPA, which issues to every sewage plant in the country a permit that spells out how much coliform bacteria and other pollutants can remain in wastewater after it has been treated. A former scientist with the Massachusetts Water Resources Authority tells me the staff in the Nut Island lab would simply ignore unfavorable test results. Their intent was not to deceive the EPA, the scientist hastens to add. "It was more like they looked at the numbers and said, 'This can't be right. Let's test it again.'" This sort of unconscious bias is common in laboratory work, and there are ways to correct for it. On Nut Island, though, the bias went uncorrected. As long as Nut Island's numbers appeared to fall within EPA limits, MDC management in Boston saw no reason to question the plant's testing regimen. To the Nut Islanders themselves, "making the permit" was proof in itself that they were alleviating the harbor's pollution.

Maintaining the alternate reality that prevailed on Nut Island required more than wishful thinking, however. It also involved strenuous denials when outsiders pointed out inconvenient facts. Consider what I learned from David Standley, who for several years was an environmental consultant to the city of Quincy. Tall and spare, with the methodical manner of a born engineer, Standley told me about the state of the plant's digester tanks in 1996.

Under the best of circumstances, sludge is nasty stuff—it scares even sewer workers—and it must be carefully tended and monitored to make sure the treatment process is on track. But everything Standley saw at the plant led him to conclude that the sludge was being handled in the most haphazard, ad hoc manner imaginable, with little concern for producing usable material. Indeed, in 1995 and 1996, the company contracted to convert Boston's sludge to fertilizer rejected 40% of the shipments from Nut Island. Clearly, there was a problem with the digesters. "I remember taking one look at the tanks' operating parameters and saying, 'This is going to die soon,'" Standley says. "When you've got volatile acids in the tanks rising and falling by 20% or more on a daily basis, with no apparent pattern, by definition something is very wrong."

Predictably enough, these misgivings found an unfriendly reception on Nut Island. "Their initial reaction," Standley says, "was hostility—they didn't like me sticking my nose into their business." Besides, they insisted, there was nothing seriously wrong with the digesters. The wide fluctuations in acidity were just one of their little idiosyncrasies. Instead of addressing the root causes of the variances, the team would improvise a quick fix, such as adding large amounts of alkali to the tanks when sample readings (which may or may not have been reliable) indicated high acidity levels.

If external events had not intervened, conditions on Nut Island would probably have continued to deteriorate until the digesters failed or some other crisis erupted. The plant's shutdown in 1997 forestalled that possibility. As part of a large-scale plan to overhaul Greater Boston's sewer system and clean up the harbor, all sewage treatment was shifted to a new, state-of-the-art facility on Deer Island. The Nut Island team was disbanded, after 30 years of effort that left the harbor no cleaner than it was in the late 1960s when the core team first came together.

The field of organizational studies is a well-established discipline with an extensive literature. Yet as far as I can determine, the syndrome that I call the Nut Island effect has, until now, gone unnamed—though not unrecognized, as I learned when I described it to other managers. Perhaps the lack of a name indicates just what a subtle and insidious thing it is; the Nut Island effect itself has flown under the radar of managers and academics just as the actions of team members go unnoticed by management. A common and longstanding feature of many public agencies and private companies, the Nut Island effect is often seen not as a pathology but as part of the normal state of affairs. I am convinced, though, that when good people are put in a situation in which they inexorably do the wrong things, it is not normal or unavoidable. It is tragic. It is a cruel waste of human passion and energy, and a deep-seated threat to an organization's mission and bottom line. That is why it is incumbent upon management to recognize the circumstances that can produce the Nut Island effect and prevent it from taking hold.

Five Steps to Failure

THE NUT ISLAND EFFECT IS A destructive organizational dynamic that pits a homogeneous, deeply committed team against its disengaged senior managers. Their conflict can be mapped as a negative feedback spiral that passes through five predictable stages.

1. Management, its attention riveted on high-visibility problems, assigns a vital, behind-the-scenes task to a team and gives that team a great deal of autonomy. Team members self-select for a strong work ethic and an aversion to the spotlight. They become adept at organizing and managing themselves, and the unit develops a proud and distinct identity.

2. Senior management takes the team's self-sufficiency for granted and ignores team members when they ask for help or try to warn of impending trouble. When trouble strikes, the team feels betrayed by management and reacts with resentment.

3. An us-against-the-world mentality takes hold in the team, as isolation heightens its sense of itself as a band of heroic outcasts. Driven by the desire to stay off management's radar screen, the team grows skillful at disguising its problems. Team members never acknowledge problems to outsiders or ask them for help. Management is all too willing to take the team's silence as a sign that all is well.

4. Management fails in its responsibility to expose the team to external perspectives and practices. As a result, the team begins to make up its own rules. The team tells itself that the rules enable it to fulfill its mission. In fact, these rules mask grave deficiencies in the team's performance.

5. Both management and the team form distorted pictures of reality that are very difficult to correct. Team members refuse to listen when well-meaning outsiders offer help or attempt to point out problems and deficiencies. Management, for its part, tells itself that no news is good news and continues to ignore team members and their task. Management and the team continue to shun each other until some external event breaks the stalemate.

How to Stop the Nut Island Effect Before It Starts

WHAT FORMS OF PREVENTIVE MEDICINE can we prescribe to help organizations avoid the Nut Island effect? Managers need to walk a fine line. The humane values and sense of commitment that distinguished the Nut Island team are precisely the virtues we want to encourage. The trick is to decouple them from the isolation and lack of external focus that breeds self-delusion, counterproductive practices, and, ultimately, failure.

On Nut Island, the workers' focus paralleled their reward system. That system evolved by default as a result of MDC headquarters' lack of interest and by explicit action from dedicated local managers. It rewarded task-driven results—avoid grit in the sedimentation tanks, keep the sludge pumps from seizing up, keep the digesters alive—rather than mission-oriented results—maximize flows to be treated through the plant, produce fertilizer-quality sludge. The Nut Island crew were heroes, but unfortunately they were fighting the wrong war. As in combat, the generals were to blame, not the enlisted personnel.

The striking persistence of the syndrome—which lingered on Nut Island until the plant was shut down in 1997, despite a decade of structural and management changes that afforded the team greater financial resources, new career options, top management support, and other opportunities—should send a strong message to corporate managers. While there are probably ways to counteract the Nut Island effect in your company, you are far better off to avoid it in the first place.

1. The first step is to install performance measures and reward structures tied to both internal operations and companywide goals. The internal links are necessary to help build the team's sense of local responsibility and camaraderie; the link to external goals ensures the proper calibration of internal operations to the corporate mission.

2. Second, senior management must establish a hands-on presence by visiting the team, holding recognition ceremonies, and leading tours of customers or employees from other parts of the organization through the site. These occasions give senior management a chance to detect early warnings of problems and they give the local team a sense that they matter and are listened to.

3. Third, team personnel must be integrated with people from other parts of the organization. This exposes the local team members to ideas and practices being used by colleagues elsewhere in the company or in other organizations. It encourages them to think in terms of the big picture.

4. Finally, outside people—managers and line workers alike—need to be rotated into the team environment. This should occur every two to three years—not so often as to be disruptive but often enough to discourage the institutionalization of bad habits. So as not to appear punitive, this rotation must be a regular feature of corporate life, not a tactic aimed at a particular group.

Originally published in March 2001
Reprint R0103C

Changing a Culture of Face Time

BILL MUNCK

Executive Summary

MARRIOTT INTERNATIONAL for many years had a deeply ingrained culture of face time—if you weren't working long hours, you weren't earning your pay. That philosophy didn't seem totally off base in an industry that provides 24/7 service, 365 days a year. But it had a price: By the mid 1990s, Marriott was finding it tough to recruit talented people, and some of its best managers were leaving, often because they wanted to spend more time with their families. "Our emphasis on face time had to go," recalls Bill Munck, a Marriott vice president for the New England region.

In this article, Munck describes how Marriott transformed its "see and be seen" culture by implementing an initiative dubbed Management Flexibility at several of its hotels. This six-month pilot program was designed to help managers strike a better balance between their work lives and their home lives—all while maintaining Marriott's high-quality customer service and its bottom-line financial results.

Munck explains how he and his leadership team took the first, relatively easy, step of eliminating redundant meetings and inefficient procedures that kept managers at the office late. The tougher task, he says, was over-hauling the fundamental way managers thought about work. Under the pilot, Marriott's message to employees was: Put in long hours when it's needed, but take off early if the work is done—and don't be shy about doing so. As a result of the program, managers are working five fewer hours per week with no drop-off in customer service levels; they report less stress and burnout; and they perceive a definite change in the culture, with less attention paid to hours worked and a greater emphasis placed on tasks accomplished.

T HE HOTEL BUSINESS IS RELENTLESS. We have to provide 24/7 service 365 days a year, and every single day is just as important as any other. So when a problem arises late on a Friday afternoon, someone has to fix it that night or over the weekend. Managers who have an attitude of "I'll get to it on Monday" don't last long in our industry.

Not surprisingly, Marriott, which prides itself on pro-viding excellent customer service, for many years had a deeply ingrained culture of "face time"—the more hours you put in, the better. The typical workweek exceeded 50 hours for many of our managers. That philosophy of "see and be seen" was effective for serving customers, but it had a price: By the mid-1990s, we were finding it

increasingly tough to recruit talented people, and some
of our best managers were leaving, often because they
wanted to spend more time with their families. Employees are the foundation of any business, but nowhere is this
more true than in the hospitality industry. Our sole product is the service we provide to families and business trav-
elers. If we were to lose our ability to attract and retain the
best managers and staff possible, we'd be in trouble.

So we knew that our emphasis on face time had to go.
In early 2000, Marriott implemented a test program
called Management Flexibility at three of the company's
hotels in the Northeast. The goal of the six-month pilot
was to help Marriott's managers strike a better balance
between their professional and personal lives, all while
maintaining the quality of our customer service and the
bottom line of our financial results. We found a lot of
quick fixes by eliminating redundant meetings and other
inefficient procedures. The tougher task was overhauling
the fundamental way we thought about work. Transforming a company's culture can be harder than changing just about anything else; people's natural inclination
is to hold on to whatever feels familiar, even when there
are better alternatives.

Because of the pilot program, managers at the three
hotels now work about five hours less per week. More
important, they perceive a definite change in our culture,
with less attention paid to hours worked and a greater
emphasis on the tasks accomplished. Furthermore,
through surveys and anecdotal evidence, we found that
those managers are experiencing significantly less job
stress and burnout. Because of this early success, Marriott
is implementing Management Flexibility at hotels in the
western, south central, and mid-Atlantic regions, and the
company plans a wider rollout in 2002. The pilot taught us

an invaluable lesson: Not only is it possible to change deep-rooted attitudes about work, but doing so can lead to improved business practices and higher efficiency.

A Moment of Revelation

About two years ago, I had one of those "bing!" moments—when the lightbulb inside your brain goes on. At the time, I was in charge of the Copley Marriott in Boston, a 1,150-room convention hotel that is one of Marriott's largest properties. I was having a one-on-one rap session with the person who oversaw our switch-board operations, a young guy in his twenties who was one of our best entry-level managers, and I asked him where he saw himself in five years. He said he really wasn't sure that he would still be with Marriott. "I'm working a minimum of 50 hours a week, sometimes 55 or 60 hours," he said. "And I commute an hour each way, so it's not just ten-hour days for me; it's 12-hour days. I don't know if I want to continue doing that, because I want to have a life outside of work."

I was taken aback—but not by the fact that he felt that way. After all, when I was his age and working long hours, I probably had the same thoughts. What struck me was how comfortable he was in telling me. Years ago, when I used to have similar rap sessions with my boss, one of the things I certainly would *not* have done was to tell him that I had doubts about staying with the company. Times have changed, I thought to myself. This generation has the gumption and actually feels comfortable enough to say, "I think you guys are out of step with what I'm looking for. I don't mind working hard, but I also want you to recognize that I have a life outside this company."

Other Marriott employees were saying the same thing, albeit in different ways. From exit interviews and from word of mouth, I knew we were losing a lot of very good managers who wanted greater flexibility in the workplace. Parents, for instance, weren't happy to be dropping off their kids at day care at 6:30 in the morning and then not picking them up again until 6 at night. Recruiting was also becoming tougher. A disturbing trend was the declining percentage of people who would accept the jobs that we offered.

So I was ready for the phone call I got in February 2000 from my boss, Bob McCarthy, who at the time was the senior vice president for the Northeast region. He had called to ask whether I'd be interested in volunteering the Copley Marriott to be a test hotel for the Management Flexibility program. The objective was for us to figure out ways that Marriott could help provide a better balance between the professional and personal lives of its managers. The success of our efforts would be judged by four criteria: reduced work hours, less job stress and burnout, no adverse impact on Marriott's financial performance, and sustained high quality of service to guests.

Bob had selected two other properties to participate in the initiative—the Peabody Marriott, a smaller hotel (260 rooms) north of Boston, and the LaGuardia Marriott, a midsize hotel (about 450 rooms) near the New York airport. The thinking was that if the pilot program was successful at these three hotels, each one a different size, then Marriott could feel reasonably confident rolling it out at its numerous properties nationwide.

Fortunately, Marriott does a pretty good job of recognizing and rewarding employees who take prudent risks. The philosophy is this: If you're not willing to try new things that have been thought out thoroughly, then you're probably not being as aggressive as you should. So when I first proposed the idea of participating in the Management Flexibility pilot to the members of my senior leadership team, I tried to convince them that we could do something important for the company—help it retain and attract the best and brightest employees. In the process, we could also get some recognition for the talent we had in our own hotel to pull the project off.

Some on my leadership team jumped on the band-wagon immediately. Others needed to talk things through. One of their questions had to do with trust: Would people abuse the program? We discussed that issue, remembering that we had voiced similar concerns when we initiated "employee empowerment" in the 1980s. Before then, if a customer in a Marriott restaurant didn't like his food, for example, the server would have to call a supervisor over to the table, which might take time, and the customer would then have to explain his problem all over again to the supervisor. After employee empowerment was introduced, the server could simply adjust the bill by herself. If people didn't abuse employee empowerment, why would they abuse Management Flexibility?

A larger issue was whether it would truly be possible for managers to cut back their hours and still get their work done without letting Marriott's high standards of quality slip. Deep down, I knew that it was. Every organization has its share of inefficiencies, and I was sure we had ours. All we had to do was find them and weed them out. Also, because our culture placed so much emphasis on the amount of time spent at the hotel, I knew that managers were sometimes hanging around at work when they didn't really need to be there. They were doing unnecessary busy work to pass the time, or they were subconsciously inflating their work, perhaps taking one hour to write a report that might have been done in half the time. To stop such practices, I knew we had to change the face-time aspect of our culture, and to accomplish that, I needed people to realize that even subtle, unintentional actions could sabotage our efforts. We could send out as many memos and talk about as many initiatives as we wanted, but if someone leaves work early one day and sees his boss glancing at her watch as he is heading out the door, that tiny gesture could send us back to square one.

Consequently, everyone on my senior leadership team—which included the director of food and beverage, the director of finance, the director of human resources, the director of engineering, and the director of room operations—was going to be crucial in setting the right tone for their departments. For some of the skeptics, I followed up our initial discussion with one-on-one meetings to talk through their doubts. Finally, after discussing all the pros and cons thoroughly, everyone agreed that the potential upside of the project far exceeded any possible downside.

Soon after news of the pilot program spread, I received a clear sign that we were headed in the right direction. A sales associate at the Peabody Marriott had resigned from the company sometime earlier, but after she heard that we were implementing a new initiative to shorten managers' hours, she asked if she could withdraw her resignation. Already the program was helping us to retain valued employees.

Following Through

As the old saying goes, actions speak louder than words. To change people's attitudes toward face time, we had to show them we were serious. First, we had an outside consulting firm, WFD, conduct a series of focus groups that included all 165 managers at the three hotels—from the entry-level managers to the senior ones. It was important that all of our managers participate; we wanted to send a clear message that this was an important project and that everyone's opinion mattered. Only then could we get an accurate picture of what we were dealing with.

The focus groups helped uncover several inefficient procedures. We learned, for instance, that Marriott managers could file certain business reports less frequently and that many of our regularly scheduled meetings were unnecessary. As an example, all the managers at the Copley Marriott used to meet monthly for a financial review of how the hotel was doing. We would go over expenses, costs, and profits, line by line, and everyone had to sit through reports from all the different departments, regardless of whether the discussion concerned them directly or not.

We also reexamined certain hotel procedures we were following, mainly out of tradition, that might have been inefficient. Our protocol dictated, for example, that front-desk managers' schedules should include a one-hour overlap with the person on the next shift. But people in the focus groups questioned that practice: Wouldn't 15 minutes be sufficient to get the next manager up-to-date?

In other cases, people were asking for certain tools to do their jobs more efficiently. For instance, lots of managers wanted access to the Internet so they could communicate with customers through e-mail. Without access to e-mail, employees were having to send proposals, contracts, sample menus, and other materials to customers by fax, overnight mail, or messenger—not exactly the most efficient way to transact business in today's hyperlinked world. And those managers who had computers wanted better IT support. At the time, if they had a problem they had to call a help desk that was staffed at our corporate headquarters in Washington, DC, sometimes having to wait until the next day before their problem could be solved. The managers wanted someone on-site who could help them right away, a person who understood their software, their systems, and the work they did in their departments.

Soon after we collected this information from the focus groups, my leadership team and I felt it was important to move quickly. Our strategy was to get some early wins to build momentum and to convince everyone that we meant business. So within a couple weeks, we started picking the "low-hanging fruit." First, we eliminated our departmental and monthly financial review meetings. I can't overstate the effect that had. Our culture was such that some of those meetings were considered sacred cows; many people assumed that Marriott would *always* have those meetings. So eliminating them was like committing a big taboo—one that was noticed by everyone. And second, over the next several weeks, we also showed people that we were willing to put our money where our mouth was by providing Internet access to those managers who needed it and by hiring an on-site systems manager. We highlighted these changes in our employee newsletters. The word spread, and people started to realize that we were indeed serious about creating an environment that would enable them to work more efficiently and get home earlier.

A Cultural Evolution

In retrospect, transforming our culture wasn't as hard as I thought it would be, mainly because people truly wanted the change. And it wasn't just employees with families; most managers expressed a desire for less stress and a better balance between their home and work lives. Nevertheless, I knew that my senior leadership team and I had to be extremely careful with how we proceeded.

First off, we wanted to make sure that people didn't mistakenly think we were talking about a 40-hour work-week. Our philosophy, which we continually emphasized through various formal and informal communications with employees, was that we were eliminating the *assumption* that you had to work at the hotel for a certain number of hours. We were no longer looking for face time. We were looking for people to be at the hotel when they needed to be and to go home when they didn't. Our message was simple: Do whatever it takes to get your job done, but be flexible in how you do it. If last week was hellish and you had to put in a lot of extra hours, but this week is much slower, then take the afternoon off and go see your son's school play or your daughter's soccer game. Don't feel bashful about doing it, and don't feel that you need to make any excuses.

Changing the work philosophy of some of our long-time managers was tricky. A few of them expected that, "If I'm your boss, you should be at work before me, and you should still be here when I leave." My leadership team and I knew we would have to work hard to change attitudes like that, and we knew we had to start at the top, with ourselves.

For me, that meant rethinking the way that I approached work. I had joined Marriott as a desk clerk almost 30 years ago, so the company's culture had pretty much become a part of me. I'm not sure that the company's emphasis on face time—that if you weren't work-

ing long hours then you weren't earning your pay—ever
made total sense to me, but Marriott was certainly a successful organization, so who was I to question it? My wife
and I have five boys, so over the years I've scooted out
early on occasion to get to one of their hockey games, but
I usually did so discreetly.

Under the Management Flexibility pilot, I made a
more concerted effort to leave early when I could and to
make sure that people were aware I was doing it. I fig-
ured if employees saw me grab my gym bag and heard
me say, as I'm walking out the door at 3:30 in the afternoon, "I'm headed home. It's been a long week. See you
later," then they would feel okay about doing the same.
People have seen me working late plenty of times. They
didn't need to be convinced that I work hard. They
needed to see that I had a life outside of work and that
when business was slow I wasn't going to hang around
just because it wasn't six o'clock yet.

About three months into the pilot, we noticed one
sure sign that things were changing: People were no
longer telling "banker's hours" jokes when others would
leave early. In the past, when someone left at five o'clock,
a coworker might remark, "Working just a half day?"
Such comments reinforced our culture of face time, and
they certainly made people feel guilty about the time
they put in. Soon, though, those jokes were being
replaced by something a lot more supportive—genuine
interest in others' outside lives: "That's great that you're
leaving early. Doing anything special? I'm taking off early
tomorrow because of my kid's baseball game."

Of course, a minimum amount of face time is essential because people need to connect with their coworkers, customers, and suppliers face-to-face. They need to

network, and so we let managers know that, although we no longer expected them to work long hours every week, we did expect them to be at the hotel every day that they were scheduled to be there.

Timely Results

During the six-month test program, we had regular reviews with our managers and other employees to track how things were going. We also conducted surveys, which suggested that there had been some dramatic improvements. For example, managers reported that before the pilot they were spending about 11.7 hours per week on "low-value" work, which was defined as the things they were required to do that added little value to Marriott's business—like having to attend certain meetings, even if it meant coming in on their scheduled days off. At the end of testing in August 2000, the time managers spent on low-value work had been slashed nearly in half to 6.8 hours per week. Overall, the managers at the three hotels said they were working an average of about five hours less each week, with the greatest time savings in the sales and marketing department; that group reported an average reduction of almost seven hours per week per manager.

Perhaps more important was the change in attitudes. Before the pilot program, 77% of managers felt that their jobs were so demanding they couldn't take adequate care of their personal and family responsibilities. At the end of the pilot, that number had plummeted to 36%. Also, the percentage of managers who felt that the emphasis at Marriott was on hours worked and not on the work accomplished plunged from 43% to 15%. (See the exhibit "Attitude Adjustment.")

One of the most important things we learned from the pilot project was that people could be just as productive—and sometimes even more so—when they worked fewer hours. How could this be? Because when they're working those fewer hours, they're extra motivated to get things done, and they don't waste any time in doing what they need to do.

Throughout the pilot program, we were extremely careful to monitor the quality of customer service to make sure our standards weren't slipping. Fortunately, Marriott already had a feedback system in place: the questionnaires that our guests routinely fill out. Our corporate headquarters compiles the data (about 70 to 80

Attitude Adjustment

During the pilot test of its Management Flexibility program, Marriott conducted employee surveys to gauge how—and if—the corporate culture was changing. The managers' responses, some of which are reported below, showed substantial changes.

The percentage of Marriott managers who said:

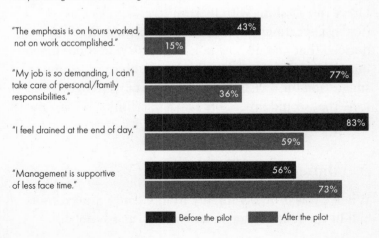

"The emphasis is on hours worked, not on work accomplished."
43%
15%

"My job is so demanding, I can't take care of personal/family responsibilities."
77%
36%

"I feel drained at the end of day."
83%
59%

"Management is supportive of less face time."
56%
73%

■ Before the pilot   ■ After the pilot

responses every month) and sends a report to us. The results showed no change in quality, which assured us that, as far as our guests were concerned, Management Flexibility was all but invisible.

We also monitored the financial impact of the pilot program and were relieved to learn that it did not adversely affect our bottom line. Although we did have additional capital expenditures (for example, providing computers and Internet access to certain managers), that cost was more than offset by gains in productivity (for instance, sales managers were able to acquire additional customers).

Furthermore, the Management Flexibility program fostered an atmosphere of open dialogue. A crucial take-home message from the pilot was that management shouldn't dictate that people do things that don't make sense; employees who are doing their jobs day in and day out often know best how to find efficient ways to do their work. After all, the best ideas don't always come from the leaders in an organization, and it's very easy for any company to slip into bad habits of doing something just because that's the way it's always been done. At Marriott, I have rap sessions with five or six associates from a particular department every Friday afternoon, and I've noticed that people now talk more freely in those meetings. Valuable information always bubbles up—often a suggestion for revising an inefficient or outdated policy—that would invariably make me think, "Wow, I'm sure glad we had this meeting."

A Balance for Everyone

When I was growing up, my friends and I played football in the fall, hockey in the winter, and baseball in

the spring. Nowadays, even young kids will specialize
in just one sport, maybe playing hockey year-round.
They go to hockey camps and practice in the summer
because they want to get a leg up so they'll get on the
best travel teams. Little Leagues have become so competitive, and parents, right or wrong, are supporting
that behavior. With my five sons, I've been just as guilty
as anyone else.

Some of that increased competitiveness has made its
way into the workplace. The attitude is this: If I work
longer and harder, and if I put off some of my vacations
and resist going home early so I can do just a little extra
work, that's going to give me an advantage over my
peers. There's some truth to that, because those extra
hours can give people additional experience that will
make them eligible for their next promotion. But does
that competitiveness then put pressure on the rest of the
organization, including people who also want to get
ahead but who want to do so with more of a balance
between their personal and professional lives? The cold
reality is that, yes, it does, and I'm not sure we're ever
going to get away from that.

Of course, the best managers are not always the
ones who work the hardest. Marriott has some weak
managers who work an awful lot of hours, and it has
other managers who are outstanding but who are
quick to leave at four o'clock if they're done for the
day. The company also has exceptionally talented
managers who are workaholics—highly motivated and
willing to make sacrifices in their personal lives to
get ahead professionally. They've chosen a lifestyle
that works for them, and that's great if they're happy
with their choices. But the big cultural change here
at Marriott is that we shouldn't expect or encourage

everyone to work the same way. After all, people who thrive both at work and in their personal lives are just as valuable—if not more so—as people who thrive only at work.

Originally published in November 2001
Reprint R0110J

The Real Reason People Won't Change

ROBERT KEGAN AND LISA LASKOW LAHEY

Executive Summary

EVERY MANAGER IS FAMILIAR with the employee who just won't change. Sometimes it's easy to see why—the employee fears a shift in power or the need to learn new skills. Other times, such resistance is far more puzzling. An employee has the skills and smarts to make a change with ease and is genuinely enthusiastic—yet, inexplicably, does nothing.

What's going on? In this article, two organizational psychologists present a surprising conclusion. Resistance to change does not necessarily reflect opposition nor is it merely a result of inertia. Instead, even as they hold a sincere commitment to change, many people are unwittingly applying productive energy toward a hidden competing commitment. The resulting internal conflict stalls the effort in what looks like resistance but is in fact a kind of personal immunity to change. An employee who's dragging his feet on a project, for example, may have an unrecognized competing commitment to avoid the even tougher assignment—one he fears he can't handle—that might follow if he delivers too successfully on the task at hand.

Without an understanding of competing commitments, attempts to change employee behavior are virtually futile. The authors outline a process for helping employees uncover their competing commitments, identify and challenge the underlying assumptions driving these commitments, and begin to change their behavior so that, ultimately, they can accomplish their goals.

Every MANAGER IS FAMILIAR with the employee who just won't change. Sometimes it's easy to see why— the employee fears a shift in power, the need to learn new skills, the stress of having to join a new team. In other cases, such resistance is far more puzzling. An employee has the skills and smarts to make a change with ease, has shown a deep commitment to the company, genuinely supports the change—and yet, inexplicably, does nothing.

What's going on? As organizational psychologists, we have seen this dynamic literally hundreds of times, and our research and analysis have recently led us to a surprising yet deceptively simple conclusion. Resistance to change does not reflect opposition, nor is it merely a result of inertia. Instead, even as they hold a sincere commitment to change, many people are unwittingly applying productive energy toward a hidden *competing commitment*. The resulting dynamic equilibrium stalls the effort in what looks like resistance but is in fact a kind of personal immunity to change.

When you, as a manager, uncover an employee's competing commitment, behavior that has seemed irrational and ineffective suddenly becomes stunningly sensible and masterful—but unfortunately, on behalf of a goal that conflicts with what you and even the employee are trying to achieve. You find out that the project leader who's dragging his feet has an unrecognized competing commitment to avoid the even tougher assignment—one he fears he can't handle—that might come his way next if he delivers too successfully on the task at hand. Or you find that the person who won't collaborate despite a passionate and sincere commitment to teamwork is equally dedicated to avoiding the conflict that naturally attends any ambitious team activity.

Helping people overcome their limitations to become more successful at work is at the very heart of effective management.

In these pages, we'll look at competing commitments in detail and take you through a process to help your employees overcome their immunity to change. The process may sound straightforward, but it is by no means quick or easy. On the contrary, it challenges the very psychological foundations upon which people function. It asks people to call into question beliefs they've long held close, perhaps since childhood. And it requires people to admit to painful, even embarrassing, feelings that they would not ordinarily disclose to others or even to themselves. Indeed, some people will opt not to disrupt their immunity to change, choosing instead to continue their fruitless struggle against their competing commitments.

As a manager, you must guide people through this exercise with understanding and sensitivity. If your employees are to engage in honest introspection and

candid disclosure, they must understand that their revelations won't be used against them. The goal of this
exploration is solely to help them become more effective,
not to find flaws in their work or character. As you support your employees in unearthing and challenging their
innermost assumptions, you may at times feel you're
playing the role of a psychologist. But in a sense, managers *are* psychologists. After all, helping people overcome their limitations to become more successful at
work is at the very heart of effective management.

We'll describe this delicate process in detail, but first
let's look at some examples of competing commitments
in action.

Shoveling Sand Against the Tide

Competing commitments cause valued employees to
behave in ways that seem inexplicable and irremediable,
and this is enormously frustrating to managers. Take the
case of John, a talented manager at a software company.
(Like all examples in this article, John's experiences are
real, although we have altered identifying features. In
some cases, we've constructed composite examples.)
John was a big believer in open communication and valued close working relationships, yet his caustic sense of
humor consistently kept colleagues at a distance. And
though he wanted to move up in the organization, his
personal style was holding him back. Repeatedly, John
was counseled on his behavior, and he readily agreed
that he needed to change the way he interacted with others in the organization. But time after time, he reverted
to his old patterns. Why, his boss wondered, did John
continue to undermine his own advancement?

As it happened, John was a person of color working as part of an otherwise all-white executive team. When he went through an exercise designed to help him unearth his competing commitments, he made a surprising discovery about himself. Underneath it all, John believed that if he became too well integrated with the team, it would threaten his sense of loyalty to his own racial group. Moving too close to the mainstream made him feel very uncomfortable, as if he were becoming "one of them" and betraying his family and friends. So when people gathered around his ideas and suggestions, he'd tear down their support with sarcasm, inevitably (and effectively) returning himself to the margins, where he was more at ease. In short, while John was genuinely committed to working well with his colleagues, he had an equally powerful competing commitment to keeping his distance.

Consider, too, a manager we'll call Helen, a rising star at a large manufacturing company. Helen had been assigned responsibility for speeding up production of the company's most popular product, yet she was spinning her wheels. When her boss, Andrew, realized that an important deadline was only two months away and she hadn't filed a single progress report, he called her into a meeting to discuss the project. Helen agreed that she was far behind schedule, acknowledging that she had been stalling in pulling together the team. But at the same time she showed a genuine commitment to making the project a success. The two developed a detailed plan for changing direction, and Andrew assumed the problem was resolved. But three weeks after the meeting, Helen still hadn't launched the team.

Why was Helen unable to change her behavior? After intense self-examination in a workshop with several of her colleagues, she came to an unexpected conclusion: Although she truly wanted the project to succeed, she had an accompanying, unacknowledged commitment to maintaining a subordinate position in relation to Andrew. At a deep level, Helen was concerned that if she succeeded, in her new role—one she was excited about and eager to undertake—she would become more a peer than a subordinate. She was uncertain whether Andrew was prepared for the turn their relationship would take. Worse, a promotion would mean that she, not Andrew, would be ultimately accountable for the results of her work—and Helen feared she wouldn't be up to the task.

Employees are almost always tremendously relieved when they discover just why they feel as if they are rolling a boulder up a hill only to have it roll back down again.

These stories shed some light on the nature of immunity to change. The inconsistencies between John's and Helen's stated goals and their actions reflect neither hypocrisy nor unspoken reluctance to change but the paralyzing effect of competing commitments. Any manager who seeks to help John communicate more effectively or Helen move her project forward, without understanding that each is also struggling unconsciously toward an opposing agenda, is shoveling sand against the tide.

Diagnosing Immunity to Change

Competing commitments aren't distressing only to the boss; they're frustrating to employees as well. People with the most sincere intentions often unwittingly create for themselves Sisyphean tasks. And they are almost always tremendously relieved when they discover just *why* they feel as if they are rolling a boulder up a hill only to have it roll back down again. Even though uncovering a competing commitment can open up a host of new concerns, the discovery offers hope for finally accomplishing the primary, stated commitment.

Based on the past 15 years of working with hundreds of managers in a variety of companies, we've developed a three-stage process to help organizations figure out what's getting in the way of change. First, managers guide employees through a set of questions designed to uncover competing commitments. Next, employees examine these commitments to determine the underlying assumptions at their core. And finally, employees start the process of changing their behavior.

We'll walk through the process fairly quickly below, but it's important to note that each step will take time. Just uncovering the competing commitment will require at least two or three hours, because people need to reflect on each question and the implications of their answers. The process of challenging competing commitments and making real progress toward overcoming immunity to change unfolds over a longer period—weeks or even months. But just getting the commitments on the table can have a noticeable effect on the decisions people make and the actions they take.

Uncovering Competing Commitments

Overcoming immunity to change starts with uncovering competing commitments. In our work, we've found that even though people keep their competing commitments well hidden, you can draw them out by asking a series of questions—as long as the employees believe that personal and potentially embarrassing disclosures won't be used inappropriately. It can be very powerful to guide people through this diagnostic exercise in a group—typically with several volunteers making their own discoveries public—so people can see that others, even the company's star performers, have competing commitments and inner contradictions of their own.

The first question we ask is, *What would you like to see changed at work, so that you could be more effective or so that work would be more satisfying?* Responses to this question are nearly always couched in a complaint— a form of communication that most managers bemoan because of its negative, unproductive tone. But complaints can be immensely useful. People complain only about the things they care about, and they complain the loudest about the things they care about most. With little effort, people can turn their familiar, uninspiring gripes into something that's more likely to energize and motivate them—a commitment, genuinely their own.

To get there, you need to ask a second question: *What commitments does your complaint imply?* A project leader we worked with, we'll call him Tom, had grumbled, "My subordinates keep me out of the loop on important developments in my project." This complaint yielded the statement, "I believe in open and candid communication." A line manager we'll call Mary lamented people's unwillingness to speak up at meetings; her complaint implied a commitment to shared decision making.

While undoubtedly sincere in voicing such commitments, people can nearly always identify some way in which they are in part responsible for preventing them from being fulfilled. Thus, the third question is: *What are* you *doing, or not doing, that is keeping your commitment from being more fully realized?* Invariably, in our experience, people can identify these undermining behaviors in just a couple of seconds. For example, Tom admitted: "When people bring me bad news, I tend to shoot the messenger." And Mary acknowledged that she didn't delegate much and that she sometimes didn't release all the information people needed in order to make good decisions.

In both cases, there may well have been other circumstances contributing to the shortfalls, but clearly both Tom and Mary were engaging in behavior that was affecting the people around them. Most people recognize this about themselves right away and are quick to say, "I need to stop doing that." Indeed, Tom had repeatedly vowed to listen more openly to potential problems that would slow his projects. However, the purpose of this exercise is not to make these behaviors disappear—at least not now. The purpose is to understand why people behave in ways that undermine their own success.

The next step, then, is to invite people to consider the consequences of forgoing the behavior. We do this by asking a fourth question: *If you imagine doing the opposite of the undermining behavior, do you detect in yourself any discomfort, worry, or vague fear?* Tom imagined himself listening calmly and openly to some bad news about a project and concluded, "I'm afraid I'll hear about a problem that I can't fix, something that I can't do anything about." And Mary? She considered allowing people more latitude and realized that, quite frankly, she feared people wouldn't make good decisions and she would be forced to carry out a strategy she thought would lead to an inferior result.

The final step is to transform that passive fear into a statement that reflects an active commitment to preventing certain outcomes. We ask, *By engaging in this undermining behavior, what worrisome outcome are you committed to preventing?* The resulting answer is the competing commitment, which lies at the very heart of a person's immunity to change. Tom admitted, "I am committed to not learning about problems I can't fix." By intimidating his staff, he prevented them from delivering bad news, protecting himself from the fear that he was not in control of the project. Mary, too, was protecting herself—in her case, against the consequences of bad decisions. "I am committed to making sure my group does not make decisions that I don't like."

Such revelations can feel embarrassing. While primary commitments nearly always reflect noble goals that people would be happy to shout from the rooftops, competing commitments are very personal, reflecting vulnerabilities that people fear will undermine how they are regarded both by others and themselves. Little wonder people keep them hidden and hasten to cover them up again once they're on the table.

But competing commitments should not be seen as weaknesses. They represent some version of self-protection, a perfectly natural and reasonable human impulse. The question is, if competing commitments are a form of self-protection, what are people protecting themselves from? The answers usually lie in what we call their *big assumptions*—deeply rooted beliefs about themselves and the world around them. These assumptions put an order to the world and at the same time suggest ways in which the world can go out of order. Competing commitments arise from these assumptions, driving behaviors unwittingly designed to keep the picture intact. (See "A Diagnostic Test for Immunity to Change.")

Examining the Big Assumption

People rarely realize they hold big assumptions because, quite simply, they accept them as reality. Often formed long ago and seldom, if ever, critically examined, big assumptions are woven into the very fabric of people's existence. (For more on the grip that big assumptions hold on people, see "Big Assumptions: How Our Perceptions Shape Our Reality" at the end of this article.) But with a little help, most people can call them up fairly easily, especially once they've identified their competing commitments. To do this, we first ask people to create the beginning of a sentence by inverting the competing commitment, and then we ask them to fill in the blank. For Tom ("I am committed to not hearing about problems I can't fix"), the big assumption turned out to be, "I assume that if I *did* hear about problems I can't fix, people would discover I'm not qualified to do my job." Mary's big assumption was that her teammates weren't as smart or experienced as she and that she'd be wasting her time and others' if she didn't maintain control. Returning to our earlier story, John's big assumption might be, "I assume that if I develop unambivalent relationships with my white coworkers, I will sacrifice my racial identity and alienate my own community."

This is a difficult process, and it doesn't happen all at once, because admitting to big assumptions makes people uncomfortable. The process can put names to very personal feelings people are reluctant to disclose, such as

A Diagnostic Test for Immunity to Change

The most important steps in diagnosing immunity to change are uncovering employees' competing commitments and unearthing their big assumptions. To do so, we ask a series of questions and record key responses in a simple grid. Below we've listed the responses for six people who went through this exercise, including the examples described in the text. The grid paints a picture of the change-immunity system, making sense of a previously puzzling dynamic.

	Stated commitment I am committed to . . .	What am I doing, or not doing, that is keeping my stated commitment from being fully realized?	Competing commitments	Big assumptions
John	. . . high quality communication with my colleagues.	Sometimes I use sarcastic humor to get my point across.	I am committed to maintaining a distance from my white colleagues.	I assume I will lose my authentic connection to my racial group if I get too integrated into the mainstream.
Helen	. . . the new initiative.	I don't push for top performance from my team members or myself; I accept mediocre products and thinking too often; I don't prioritize.	I am committed to not upsetting my relationship with my boss by leaving the mentee role.	I assume my boss will stop supporting me if I move toward becoming his peer; I assume that I don't have what it takes to successfully carry out a cutting-edge project.
Tom	. . . hearing from my subordinates and maximizing the flow of information into my office.	I don't ask questions or ask to be kept in the loop on sensitive or delicate matters; I shoot the messenger when I hear bad news.	I am committed to not learning about things I can't do anything about.	I assume as a leader I should be able to address all problems; I assume I will be seen as incompetent if I can't solve all problems that come up.

Mary	. . . distributed leadership by enabling people to make decisions.	I don't delegate enough; I don't pass on the necessary information to the people I distribute leadership to.	I am committed to having things go my way, to being in control, and to ensuring that the work is done to my high standards.	I assume that other people will waste my time and theirs if I don't step in; I assume others aren't as smart as I am.
Bill	. . . being a team player.	I don't collaborate enough; I make unilateral decisions too often; I don't really take people's input into account.	I am committed to being the one who gets the credit and to avoiding the frustration or conflict that comes with collaboration.	I assume that no one will appreciate me if I am not seen as the source of success; I assume nothing good will come of my being frustrated or in conflict.
Jane	. . . turning around my department.	Too often I let things slide; I'm not proactive enough in getting people to follow through with their tasks.	I am committed to not setting full sail until I have a clear map of how we get our department from here to there.	I assume that if I take my group out into deep waters and discover I am unable to get us to the other side, I will be seen as an incompetent leader who is undeserving of trust or responsibility.

deep-seated fears or insecurities, highly discouraging or simplistic views of human nature, or perceptions of their own superior abilities or intellect. Unquestioning acceptance of a big assumption anchors and sustains an immune system: A competing commitment makes all the sense in the world, and the person continues to engage in behaviors that support it, albeit unconsciously, to the detriment of his or her "official," stated commitment. Only by bringing big assumptions to light can people finally challenge their assumptions and recognize why they are engaging in seemingly contradictory behavior.

Questioning the Big Assumption

Once people have identified their competing commitments and the big assumptions that sustain them, most are prepared to take some immediate action to overcome their immunity. But the first part of the process involves observation, not action, which can be frustrating for high achievers accustomed to leaping into motion to solve problems. Let's take a look at the steps in more detail.

Step 1: Notice and record current behavior. Employees must first take notice of what does and doesn't happen as a consequence of holding big assumptions to be true. We specifically ask people *not* to try to make any changes in their thinking or behavior at this time but just to become more aware of their actions in relation to their big assumptions. This gives people the opportunity to develop a better appreciation for how and in what contexts big assumptions influence their lives. John, for example, who had assumed that working well with his white colleagues would estrange him from his ethnic group, saw that he had missed an opportunity to get involved in an exciting, high-profile initiative because he had mocked the idea when it first came up in a meeting.

Step 2: Look for contrary evidence. Next, employees must look actively for experiences that might cast doubt on the validity of their big assumptions. Because big assumptions are held as fact, they actually inform what people see, leading them to systematically (but unconsciously) attend to certain data and avoid or ignore other data. By asking people to search specifically for experiences that would cause them to question their big assumptions, we help them see that they have been filtering out certain types of information—information that could weaken the grip of the big assumptions.

When John looked around him, he considered for the first time that an African-American manager in another department had strong working relationships with her mostly white colleagues, yet seemed not to have compromised her personal identity. He also had to admit that when he had been thrown onto an urgent task force the year before, he had worked many hours alongside his white colleagues and had found the experience satisfying; he had felt none of his usual ambivalence.

Step 3: Explore the history. In this step, we invite people to become the "biographers" of their big assumptions: How and when did the assumptions first take hold? How long have they been around? What have been some of their critical turning points?

Typically, this step leads people to earlier life experiences, almost always to times before their current jobs and relationships with current coworkers. This reflection usually makes people feel dissatisfied with the foundations of their big assumptions, especially when they see that these ideas have accompanied them to their current positions and have been coloring their experiences for many years. Recently, a CEO expressed astonishment as she realized she'd been applying the same self-protective stance in her work that she'd developed during a difficult divorce years before. Just as commonly, as was the case for John, people trace their big assumptions to early experiences with parents, siblings, or friends. Understanding the circumstances that influenced the formation of the assumptions can free people to consider whether these beliefs apply to their present selves.

Step 4: Test the assumption. This step entails creating and running a modest test of the big assumption. This is the first time we ask people to consider making changes in their behavior. Each employee should come up with a scenario and run it by a partner who serves as a sounding board. (Left to their own devices, people tend to create tests that are either too risky or so tentative that they don't actually challenge the assumption and in fact reaffirm its validity.) After conferring with a partner, John, for instance, volunteered to join a short-term committee looking at his department's process for evaluating new product ideas. Because the team would dissolve after a month, he would be able to extricate himself fairly quickly if he grew too uncomfortable with the relationships. But the experience would force him to spend a significant amount of time with several of his white colleagues during that month and would provide him an opportunity to test his sense of the real costs of being a full team member.

Step 5: Evaluate the results. In the last step, employees evaluate the test results, evaluate the test itself, design and run new tests, and eventually question the big assumptions. For John, this meant signing up for other initiatives and making initial social overtures to white coworkers. At the same time, by engaging in volunteer efforts within his community outside of work, he made sure that his ties to his racial group were not compromised.

It is worth noting that revealing a big assumption doesn't necessarily mean it will be exposed as false. But even if a big assumption does contain an element of truth, an individual can often find more effective ways to operate once he or she has had a chance to challenge the assumption and its hold on his or her behavior. Indeed, John found a way to support the essence of his competing commitment—to maintain his bond with his racial group—while minimizing behavior that sabotaged his other stated commitments. (See "Getting Groups to Change" at the end of this article.)

Uncovering Your Own Immunity

As you go through this process with your employees, remember that managers are every bit as susceptible to change immunity as employees are, and your competing commitments and big assumptions can have a significant impact on the people around you. Returning once more to Helen's story: When we went through this exercise with her boss, Andrew, it turned out that he was harboring some contradictions of his own. While he was committed to the success of his subordinates, Andrew at some level assumed that he alone could meet his high standards, and as a result he was laboring under a competing commitment to maintain absolute control over his projects. He was unintentionally communicating this lack of confidence to his subordinates—including Helen—in subtle ways. In the end, Andrew's and Helen's competing commitments were, without their knowledge, mutually reinforcing, keeping Helen dependent on Andrew and allowing Andrew to control her projects.

Helen and Andrew are still working through this process, but they've already gained invaluable insight into their behavior and the ways they are impeding their own progress. This may seem like a small step, but bringing these issues to the surface and confronting them head-on is challenging and painful—yet tremendously effective. It allows managers to see, at last, what's really going on when people who are genuinely committed to change nonetheless dig in their heels. It's not about identifying unproductive behavior and systematically making plans to correct it, as if treating symptoms would cure a disease. It's not about coaxing or cajoling or even giving poor performance reviews. It's about understanding the complexities of people's behavior, guiding them through a productive process to bring their competing commitments to the surface, and helping them cope with the inner conflict that is preventing them from achieving their goals.

Big Assumptions: How Our Perceptions Shape Our Reality

BIG ASSUMPTIONS REFLECT the very human manner in which we invent or shape a picture of the world and then take our inventions for reality. This is easiest to see in children. The delight we take in their charming distortions is a kind of celebration that they are actively making sense of the world, even if a bit eccentrically. As one story goes, two youngsters had been learning about Hindu culture and were taken with a representation of the universe in which the world sits atop a giant elephant, and the elephant sits atop an even more giant turtle. "I wonder what the turtle sits on," says one of the children. "I think from then on," says the other, "it's turtles all the way down."

But deep within our amusement may lurk a note of condescension, an implication that this is what distinguishes children from grown-ups. Their meaning-making is subject to youthful distortions, we assume. Ours represents an accurate map of reality.

But does it? Are we really finished discovering, once we have reached adulthood, that our maps don't match the territory? The answer is clearly no. In our 20 years of longitudinal and cross-sectional research, we've discovered that adults must grow into and out of several qualitatively different views of the world if they are to master the challenges of their life experiences (see Robert Kegan, *In Over Our Heads*, Harvard University Press, 1994).

A woman we met from Australia told us about her experience living in the United States for a year. "Not only do you drive on the wrong side of the street over here," she said, "your steering wheels are on the wrong side, too. I would routinely pile into the right side of the car to drive off, only to discover I needed to get out and walk over to the other side.

"One day," she continued, "I was thinking about six different things, and I got into the right side of the car, took out my keys, and was prepared to drive off. I looked up and thought to myself, 'My God, here in the violent and lawless United States, they are even stealing *steering wheels!*'"

Of course, the countervailing evidence was just an arm's length to her left, but—and this is the main point—*why should she look?* Our big assumptions create a disarming and deluding sense of certainty. If we know where a steering wheel belongs, we are unlikely to look for it some place else. If we know what our company, department, boss, or subordinate can and can't do, why should we look for countervailing data—even if it is just an arm's length away?

Getting Groups to Change

ALTHOUGH COMPETING commitments and big assumptions tend to be deeply personal, groups are just as susceptible as individuals to the dynamics of immunity to change. Face-to-face teams, departments, and even companies as a whole can fall prey to inner contradictions that "protect" them from significant changes they may genuinely strive for. The leadership team of a video production company, for instance, enjoyed a highly collaborative, largely flat organizational structure. A year before we met the group, team members had undertaken a planning process that led them to a commitment of which they were unanimously in favor: In order to ensure that the company would grow in the way the team wished, each of the principals would take responsibility for aggressively overseeing a distinct market segment.

The members of the leadership team told us they came out of this process with a great deal of momentum. They knew which markets to target, they had formed some concrete plans for moving forward, and they had clearly assigned accountability for each market. Yet a year later, the group had to admit it had accomplished very little, despite the enthusiasm. There were lots of rational explanations: "We were unrealistic; we thought we could do new things and still have time to keep meeting our present obligations." "We didn't pursue new clients aggressively enough." "We tried new things but gave up too quickly if they didn't immediately pay off."

Efforts to overcome these barriers—to pursue clients more aggressively, for instance—didn't work because they didn't get to the cause of the unproductive behavior. But by seeing the team's explanations as a potential window into the bigger competing commitment, we were able to help the group better understand its predicament. We asked, "Can you identify even the vaguest fear or worry about what might happen if you *did* more aggressively pursue the new markets? Or if you reduced some of your present activity on behalf of building the new business?" Before long, a different discourse began to emerge, and the other half of a striking groupwide contradiction came into view: The principals were worried that pursuing the plan would drive them apart functionally and emotionally.

"We now realize we are also committed to preserving the noncompetitive, intellectually rewarding, and cocreative spirit of our corporate enterprise," they concluded. On behalf of this commitment, the team members had to commend themselves on how "noncompetitively" and "cocreatively" they were finding ways to undermine the strategic plans they still believed were the best route to the company's future success. The team's big assumptions? "We assumed that pursuing the target-market strategy, with each of us taking aggressive responsibility for a given segment, would create the 'silos' we have long happily avoided and would leave us more isolated from one another. We also assumed the strategy would make us more competitively disposed toward one another." Whether or not the assumptions were true, they would have continued to block the group's efforts until they were brought to light. In fact, as the group came to discover, there were a variety of moves that would allow the leadership team to preserve a genuinely collaborative collegiality while pursuing the new corporate strategy.

Originally published in November 2001
Reprint R0110E

Radical Change, the Quiet Way

DEBRA E. MEYERSON

Executive Summary

AT SOME POINT, many managers yearn to confront assumptions, practices, or values in their organizations that they feel are counterproductive or even downright wrong. Yet they can face an uncomfortable dilemma: If they speak out too loudly, resentment may build toward them; if they remain silent, resentment will build inside them. Is there any way, then, to rock the boat without falling out of it?

In 15 years of research, professor Debra Meyerson has observed hundreds of professionals who have dealt with this problem by working behind the scenes, engaging in a subtle form of grassroots leadership. She calls them "tempered radicals" because they effect significant changes in moderate ways.

Meyerson has identified four incremental approaches that managers can quietly use to create lasting cultural change. Most subtle is "disruptive self-expression" in dress, office decor, or behavior which can slowly change an unproductive atmosphere as people increasingly notice and emulate it. By using "verbal jujitsu," an individual can redirect the force of an intensive statement or action to improve the situation. "Variable-term opportunists" spot, create, and capitalize on short- and long-term chances for change. And through "strategic alliance building," an individual can join with others to promote change with more force. By adjusting these approaches to time and circumstance, tempered radicals work subtly but effectively to alter the status quo.

In so doing, they exercise a form of leadership that is more modest and less visible than traditional forms—yet no less significant. Top managers who want to create cultural or organizational change—perhaps they're moving tradition-bound businesses down new roads—should seek out these tempered radicals, for they are masters at transforming organizations from the grass roots.

AT ONE POINT OR ANOTHER, many managers experience a pang of conscience—a yearning to confront the basic or hidden assumptions, interests, practices, or values within an organization that they feel are stodgy, unfair, even downright wrong. A vice president wishes that more people of color would be promoted. A partner at a consulting firm thinks new MBAs are being so overworked that their families are hurting. A senior manager suspects his company, with some extra cost, could be kinder to the environment. Yet many people who want to drive changes like these face an uncomfortable dilemma. If they speak out too loudly, resentment builds toward them; if they play by the rules and remain silent, resentment builds inside them. Is there any way, then, to rock the boat without falling out of it?

Over the past 15 years, I have studied hundreds of professionals who spend the better part of their work lives trying to answer this question. Each one of the people I've studied differs from the organizational status quo in some way—in values, race, gender, or sexual preference, perhaps (see "How the Research Was Done" at the end of this article). They all see things a bit differently from the "norm." But despite feeling at odds with aspects of the prevailing culture, they genuinely like their jobs and want to continue to succeed in them, to effectively use their differences as the impetus for constructive change. They believe that direct, angry confrontation will get them nowhere, but they don't sit by and allow frustration to fester. Rather, they work quietly to challenge prevailing wisdom and gently provoke their organizational cultures to adapt. I call such change agents *tempered radicals* because they work to effect significant changes in moderate ways.

In so doing, they exercise a form of leadership within organizations that is more localized, more diffuse, more modest, and less visible than traditional forms—yet no less significant. In fact, top executives seeking to institute cultural or organizational change—who are, perhaps, moving tradition-bound organizations down new roads or who are concerned about reaping the full potential of marginalized employees—might do well to seek out these tempered radicals, who may be hidden deep within their own organizations. Because such individuals are both dedicated to their companies and masters at changing organizations at the grassroots level, they can prove extremely valuable in helping top managers to

identify fundamental causes of discord, recognize alternative perspectives, and adapt to changing needs and
circumstances. In addition, tempered radicals, given support from above and a modicum of room to experiment,
can prove to be excellent leaders. (For more on management's role in fostering tempered radicals, see "Tempered Radicals as Everyday Leaders" at the end of this
article.)

Since the actions of tempered radicals are not, by
design, dramatic, their leadership may be difficult to recognize. How, then, do people who run organizations,
who want to nurture this diffuse source of cultural adaptation, find and develop these latent leaders? One way is
to appreciate the variety of modes in which tempered
radicals operate, learn from them, and support their
efforts.

To navigate between their personal beliefs and the
surrounding cultures, tempered radicals draw principally
on a spectrum of incremental approaches, including four
I describe here. I call these *disruptive self-expression, verbal jujitsu, variable-term opportunism,* and *strategic
alliance building.* Disruptive self-expression, in which an
individual simply acts in a way that feels personally right
but that others notice, is the most inconspicuous way to
initiate change. Verbal jujitsu turns an insensitive statement, action, or behavior back on itself. Variable-term
opportunists spot, create, and capitalize on short- and
long-term opportunities for change. And with the help of
strategic alliances, an individual can push through
change with more force. (See the exhibit "A Spectrum of
Tempered Change Strategies.")

Each of these approaches can be used in many ways,
with plenty of room for creativity and wit. Self-expression
can be done with a whisper; an employee who seeks more

racial diversity in the ranks might wear her dashiki to
company parties. Or it can be done with a roar; that same
employee might wear her dashiki to the office every day.
Similarly, a person seeking stricter environmental policies might build an alliance by enlisting the help of one
person, the more powerful the better. Or he might post his
stance on the company intranet and actively seek a host
of supporters. Taken together, the approaches form a
continuum of choices from which tempered radicals draw
at different times and in various circumstances.

But before looking at the approaches in detail, it's
worth reconsidering, for a moment, the ways in which
cultural change happens in the workplace.

A Spectrum of Tempered Change Strategies

*The tempered radical's spectrum of strategies is anchored on the left by
disruptive self-expression: subtle acts of private, individual style. A slightly
more public form of expression, verbal jujitsu, turns the opposition's negative expression or behavior into opportunities for change. Further along
the spectrum, the tempered radical uses variable-term opportunism to recognize and act on short- and long-term chances to motivate others. And
through strategic alliance building, the individual works directly with others to bring about more extensive change. The more conversations an
individual's action inspires and the more people it engages, the stronger
the impetus toward change becomes.*

*In reality, people don't apply the strategies in the spectrum sequen-
tially or even necessarily separately. Rather, these tools blur and overlap.
Tempered radicals remain flexible in their approach, "heating up" or
"cooling off" each as conditions warrant.*

Disruptive self-expression	Verbal jujitsu	Variable-term opportunism	Strategic alliance building
Most Personal (Single individual)			**Most Public** (Working with others)

How Organizations Change

Research has shown that organizations change primarily in two ways: through drastic action and through evolutionary adaptation. In the former case, change is discontinuous and often forced on the organization or mandated by top management in the wake of major technological innovations, by a scarcity or abundance of critical resources, or by sudden changes in the regulatory, legal, competitive, or political landscape. Under such circumstances, change may happen quickly and often involves significant pain. Evolutionary change, by contrast, is gentle, incremental, decentralized, and over time produces a broad and lasting shift with less upheaval.

The power of evolutionary approaches to promote cultural change is the subject of frequent discussion. For instance, in "We Don't Need Another Hero" (HBR, September 2001), Joseph L. Badaracco, Jr., asserts that the most effective moral leaders often operate beneath the radar, achieving their reforms without widespread notice. Likewise, tempered radicals gently and continually push against prevailing norms, making a difference in small but steady ways and setting examples from which others can learn. The changes they inspire are so incremental that they barely merit notice—which is exactly why they work so well. Like drops of water, these approaches are innocuous enough in themselves. But over time and in accumulation, they can erode granite.

Consider, for example, how a single individual slowly—but radically—altered the face of his organization. Peter Grant[1] was a black senior executive who held some 18 positions as he moved up the ladder at a large West Coast bank. When he first joined the company as a manager, he was one of only a handful of people of color on the professional staff. Peter had a private, long-term goal: to bring more women and racial minorities into the fold and help them succeed. Throughout his 30-year career running the company's local banks, regional offices, and corporate operations, one of his chief responsibilities was to hire new talent. Each time he had the opportunity, Peter attempted to hire a highly qualified member of a minority. But he did more than that—every time he hired someone, he asked that person to do the same. He explained to the new recruits the importance of hiring women and people of color and why it was their obligation to do likewise.

Whenever minority employees felt frustrated by bias, Peter would act as a supportive mentor. If they threatened to quit, he would talk them out of it. "I know how you feel, but think about the bigger picture here," he'd say. "If you leave, nothing here will change." His example inspired viral behavior in others. Many stayed and hired other minorities; those who didn't carried a commitment to hire minorities into their new companies. By the time Peter retired, more than 3,500 talented minority and female employees had joined the bank.

Peter was the most tempered, yet the most effective, of radicals. For many years, he endured racial slurs and demeaning remarks from colleagues. He waited longer than his peers for promotions; each time he did move up he was told the job was too big for him and he was lucky to have gotten it. "I worked my rear end off to make them comfortable with me," he said, late in his career. "It wasn't *luck*." He was often angry, but lashing out would have been the path of least emotional resistance. So without attacking the system, advancing a bold vision, or wielding great power, Peter chipped away at the organization's demographic base using the full menu of change strategies described below.

Disruptive Self-Expression

At the most tempered end of the change continuum is the kind of self-expression that quietly disrupts others' expectations. Whether waged as a deliberate act of protest or merely as a personal demonstration of one's values, disruptive self-expression in language, dress, office decor, or behavior can slowly change the atmosphere at work. Once people take notice of the expression, they begin to talk about it. Eventually, they may feel brave enough to try the same thing themselves. The more people who talk about the transgressive act or repeat it, the greater the cultural impact.

Consider the case of John Ziwak, a manager in the business development group of a high-growth computer components company. As a hardworking business school graduate who'd landed a plum job, John had every intention of working 80-hour weeks on the fast track to the top. Within a few years, he married a woman who also held a demanding job; soon, he became the father of two. John found his life torn between the competing responsibilities of home and work. To balance the two, John shifted his work hours—coming into the office earlier in the morning so that he could leave by 6 pm. He rarely scheduled late-afternoon meetings and generally refused to take calls at home in the evening between 6:30 and 9. As a result, his family life improved, and he felt much less stress, which in turn improved his performance at work.

Even the smallest forms of disruptive self-expression can be exquisitely powerful.

At first, John's schedule raised eyebrows; availability was, after all, an unspoken key indicator of commitment to the company. "If John is unwilling to stay past 6," his boss wondered, "is he really committed to his job? Why should I promote him when others are willing and able to work all the time?" But John always met his performance expectations, and his boss didn't want to lose him. Over time, John's colleagues adjusted to his schedule. No one set up conference calls or meetings involving him after 5. One by one, other employees began adopting John's "6 o'clock rule"; calls at home, particularly during dinner hour, took place only when absolutely necessary. Although the 6 o'clock rule was never formalized, it nonetheless became par for the course in John's department. Some of John's colleagues continued to work late, but they all appreciated these changes in work practice and easily accommodated them. Most people in the department felt more, not less, productive during the day as they adapted their work habits to get things done more efficiently—for example, running meetings on schedule and monitoring interruptions in their day. According to John's boss, the employees appreciated the newfound balance in their lives, and productivity in the department did not suffer in the least.

Tempered radicals know that even the smallest forms of disruptive self-expression can be exquisitely powerful. The story of Dr. Frances Conley offers a case in point. By 1987, Dr. Conley had already established herself as a leading researcher and neurosurgeon at Stanford Medical School and the Palo Alto Veteran's Administration hospital. But as one of very few women in the profession, she struggled daily to maintain her feminine identity in a macho profession and her integrity amid gender discrimination. She had to keep her cool when, for example, in

the middle of directing a team of residents through complicated brain surgery, a male colleague would stride into
the operating room to say, "Move over, honey." "Not only
did that undermine my authority and expertise with the
team," Dr. Conley recalled later, "but it was unwar-
ranted—and even dangerous. That kind of thing would
happen all the time."

Despite the frustration and anger she felt, Dr. Conley
at that time had no intention of making a huge issue of
her gender. She didn't want the fact that she was a
woman to compromise her position, or vice versa. So she
expressed herself in all sorts of subtle ways, including in
what she wore. Along with her green surgical scrubs, she
donned white lace ankle socks—an unequivocal expression of her femininity. In itself, wearing lace ankle socks
could hardly be considered a Gandhian act of civil dis-
obedience. The socks merely said, "I can be a neurosurgeon and be feminine." But they spoke loudly enough in
the stolid masculinity of the surgical environment, and,
along with other small actions on her part, they sparked
conversation in the hospital. Nurses and female residents
frequently commented on Dr. Conley's style. "She is as
demanding as any man and is not afraid to take them
on," they would say, in admiration. "But she is also a
woman and not ashamed of it."

Ellen Thomas made a comparable statement with her
hair. As a young African-American consultant in a technical services business, she navigated constantly
between organizational pressures to fit in and her personal desire to challenge norms that made it difficult for
her to be herself. So from the beginning of her employ-
ment, Ellen expressed herself by wearing her hair in neat
cornrow braids. For Ellen, the way she wore her hair was
not just about style; it was a symbol of her racial identity.

Once, before making an important client presentation, a senior colleague advised Ellen to unbraid her hair
"to appear more professional." Ellen was miffed, but she
didn't respond. Instead, she simply did not comply. Once
the presentation was over and the client had been
signed, she pulled her colleague aside. "I want you to
know why I wear my hair this way," she said calmly. "I'm
a black woman, and I happen to like the style. And as you
just saw," she smiled, "my hairstyle has nothing to do
with my ability to do my job."

Does leaving work at 6 pm or wearing lacy socks or
cornrows force immediate change in the culture? Of
course not; such acts are too modest. But disruptive self-
expression does do two important things. First, it reinforces the tempered radical's sense of the importance of
his or her convictions. These acts are self-affirming. Second, it pushes the status quo door slightly ajar by intro-
ducing an alternative modus operandi. Whether they are
subtle, unspoken, and recognizable by only a few or
vocal, visible, and noteworthy to many, such acts, in
aggregation, can provoke real reform.

Verbal Jujitsu

Like most martial arts, jujitsu involves taking a force
coming at you and redirecting it to change the situation.
Employees who practice verbal jujitsu react to undesir-
able, demeaning statements or actions by turning them
into opportunities for change that others will notice.

One form of verbal jujitsu involves calling attention to
the opposition's own rhetoric. I recall a story told by a
man named Tom Novak, an openly gay executive who
worked in the San Francisco offices of a large financial
services institution. As Tom and his colleagues began

seating themselves around a table for a meeting in a senior executive's large office, the conversation briefly turned to the topic of the upcoming Gay Freedom Day parade and to so-called gay lifestyles in general. Joe, a colleague, said loudly, "I can appreciate that some people choose a gay lifestyle. I just don't understand why they have to flaunt it in people's faces."

Stung, Tom was tempted to keep his mouth shut and absorb the injury, but that would have left him resentful and angry. He could have openly condemned Joe's bias, but that would have made him look defensive and self-righteous. Instead, he countered Joe with an altered version of Joe's own argument, saying calmly, "I know what you mean, Joe. I'm just wondering about that big picture of your wife on your desk. There's nothing wrong with being straight, but it seems that you are the one announcing your sexuality." Suddenly embarrassed, Joe responded with a simple, "Touché."

Managers can use verbal jujitsu to prevent talented employees, and their valuable contributions, from becoming inadvertently marginalized. That's what happened in the following story. Brad Williams was a sales manager at a high-technology company. During a meeting one day, Brad noticed that Sue, the new marketing director, had tried to interject a few comments, but everything she said was routinely ignored. Brad waited for the right moment to correct the situation. Later on in the meeting, Sue's colleague George raised similar concerns about distributing the new business's products outside the country. The intelligent remark stopped all conversation. During the pause, Brad jumped in: "That's an important idea," he said. "I'm glad George picked up on Sue's concerns. Sue, did George correctly capture what you were thinking?"

With this simple move, Brad accomplished a number of things. First, by indirectly showing how Sue had been silenced and her idea co-opted, he voiced an unspoken fact. Second, by raising Sue's visibility, he changed the power dynamic in the room. Third, his action taught his colleagues a lesson about the way they listened—and didn't. Sue said that after that incident she was no longer passed over in staff meetings.

In practicing verbal jujitsu, both Tom and Brad displayed considerable self-control and emotional intelligence. They listened to and studied the situation at hand, carefully calibrating their responses to disarm without harming. In addition, they identified the underlying issues (sexual bias, the silencing of newcomers) without sounding accusatory and relieved unconscious tensions by voicing them. In so doing, they initiated small but meaningful changes in their colleagues' assumptions and behavior.

Variable-Term Opportunism

Like jazz musicians, who build completely new musical experiences from old standards as they go along, tempered radicals must be creatively open to opportunity. In the short-term, that means being prepared to capitalize on serendipitous circumstances; in the long-term, it often means something more proactive. The first story that follows illustrates the former case; the second is an example of the latter.

Tempered radicals like Chris Morgan know that rich opportunities for reform can often appear suddenly, like a $20 bill found on a sidewalk. An investment manager in the audit department of a New York conglomerate, Chris made a habit of doing whatever he could to reduce waste.

To save paper, for example, he would single-space his documents and put them in a smaller font before pressing the "Print" button, and he would use both sides of the paper. One day, Chris noticed that the company cafeteria packaged its sandwiches in Styrofoam boxes that people opened and immediately tossed. He pulled the cafeteria manager aside. "Mary," he said with a big smile, "those turkey-on-focaccia sandwiches look delicious today! I was wondering, though . . . would it be possible to wrap sandwiches only when people asked you to?" By making this very small change, Chris pointed out, the cafeteria would save substantially on packaging costs.

Chris gently rocked the boat by taking the following steps. First, he picked low-hanging fruit, focusing on something that could be done easily and without causing a lot of stir. Next, he attacked the problem not by criticizing Mary's judgment but by enrolling her in his agenda (praising her tempting sandwiches, then making a gentle suggestion). Third, he illuminated the advantages of the proposed change by pointing out the benefits to the cafeteria. And he started a conversation that, through Mary, spread to the rest of the cafeteria staff. Finally, he inspired others to action: Eventually, the cafeteria staff identified and eliminated 12 other wasteful practices.

Add up enough conversations and inspire enough people and, sooner or later, you get real change. A senior executive named Jane Adams offers a case in point. Jane was hired in 1995 to run a 100-person, mostly male software-development division in an extremely fast-growing, pre-IPO technology company. The CEO of the company was an autocrat who expected his employees to emulate his dog-eat-dog management style. Although Jane was new to the job and wanted very much to fit in and succeed, turf wars and command-and-control tactics were anathema to her. Her style was more collaborative; she believed in sharing power. Jane knew that she could not attack the company's culture by arguing with the CEO; rather, she took charge of her own division and ran it her own way. To that end, she took every opportunity to share power with subordinates. She instructed each of her direct reports to delegate responsibility as much as possible. Each time she heard about someone taking initiative in making a decision, she would praise that person openly before his or her manager. She encouraged people to take calculated risks and to challenge her.

When asked to give high-visibility presentations to the company's executive staff, she passed the opportunities to those who had worked directly on the project. At first, senior executives raised their eyebrows, but Jane assured them that the presenter would deliver. Thus, her subordinates gained experience and won credit that, had they worked for someone else, they would likely never have received.

Occasionally, people would tell Jane that they noticed a refreshing contrast between her approach and the company's prevailing one. "Thanks, I'm glad you noticed," she would say with a quiet smile. Within a year, she saw that several of her own direct reports began themselves to lead in a more collaborative manner. Soon, employees from other divisions, hearing that Jane's was one of the best to work for, began requesting transfers. More important, Jane's group became known as one of the best training grounds and Jane as one of the best teachers and mentors of new talent. Nowhere else did people get the experience, responsibility, and confidence that she cultivated in her employees.

For Chris Morgan, opportunity was short-term and serendipitous. For Jane Adams, opportunity was more

long-term, something to be mined methodically. In both
cases, though, remaining alert to such variable-term
opportunities and being ready to capitalize on them
were essential.

Strategic Alliance Building

So far, we have seen how tempered radicals, more or less
working alone, can effect change. What happens when
these individuals work with allies? Clearly, they gain a
sense of legitimacy, access to resources and contacts,
technical and task assistance, emotional support, and
advice. But they gain much more—the power to move
issues to the forefront more quickly and directly than
they might by working alone.

When one enlists the help of like-minded, similarly
tempered coworkers, the strategic alliance gains clout.
That's what happened when a group of senior women at
a large professional services firm worked with a group of
men sympathetic to their cause. The firm's executive
management asked the four-woman group to find out
why it was so hard for the company to keep female consultants on staff. In the course of their investigation, the
women discussed the demanding culture of the firm: a
70-hour work week was the norm, and most consultants
spent most of their time on the road, visiting clients. The
only people who escaped this demanding schedule were
part-time consultants, nearly all of whom happened to
be women with families. These part-timers were evaluated according to the same performance criteria—
including the expectation of long hours—as full-time
workers. Though many of the part-timers were talented
contributors, they consistently failed to meet the time
criterion and so left the company. To correct the problem, the senior women first gained the ear of several

executive men who, they knew, regretted missing time with their own families. The men agreed that this was a problem and that the company could not continue to bleed valuable talent. They signed on to help address the issue and, in a matter of months, the evaluation system was adjusted to make success possible for all workers, regardless of their hours.

Tempered radicals don't allow preconceived notions about "the opposition" to get in their way. Indeed, they understand that those who represent the majority perspective are vitally important to gaining support for their cause. Paul Wielgus quietly started a revolution at his company by effectively persuading the opposition to join him. In 1991, Allied Domecq, the global spirits company whose brands include Courvoisier and Beefeater, hired Paul as a marketing director in its brewing and wholesaling division. Originally founded in 1961 as the result of a merger of three British brewing and pub-owning companies, the company had inherited a bureaucratic culture. Tony Hales, the CEO, recognized the need for dramatic change inside the organization and appreciated Paul's talent and fresh perspective. He therefore allowed Paul to quit his marketing job, report directly to the CEO, and found a nine-person learning and training department that ran programs to help participants shake off stodgy thinking and boost their creativity. Yet despite the department's blessing from on high and a two-year record of success, some managers thought of it as fluff. In fact, when David, a senior executive from the internal audit department, was asked to review cases of unnecessary expense, he called Paul on the carpet.

Paul's strategy was to treat David not as a threat but as an equal, even a friend. Instead of being defensive during the meeting, Paul used the opportunity to sell his program. He explained that the trainers worked first with individuals to help unearth their personal values, then worked with them in teams to develop new sets of group values that they all believed in. Next, the trainers aligned these personal and departmental values with those of the company as a whole. "You wouldn't believe the changes, David," he said, enthusiastically. "People come out of these workshops feeling so much more excited about their work. They find more meaning and purpose in it, and as a consequence are happier and much more productive. They call in sick less often, they come to work earlier in the morning, and the ideas they produce are much stronger." Once David understood the value of Paul's program, the two began to talk about holding the training program in the internal audit department itself.

Paul's refusal to be frightened by the system, his belief in the importance of his work, his search for creative and collaborative solutions, his lack of defensiveness with an adversary, and his ability to connect with the auditor paved the way for further change at Allied Domecq. Eventually, the working relationship the two men had formed allowed the internal audit department to transform its image as a policing unit into something more positive. The new Audit Services department came to be known as a partner, rather than an enforcer, in the organization as a whole. And as head of the newly renamed department, David became a strong supporter of Paul's work.

Tempered radicals understand that people who represent the majority perspective can be important allies in more subtle ways as well. In navigating the course between their desire to undo the status quo and the organizational requirements to uphold it, tempered radicals benefit from the advice of insiders who know just how hard to push. When a feminist who wants to change the way her company treats women befriends a conservative Republican man, she knows he can warn her of political minefields. When a Latino manager wants his company to put a Spanish-language version of a manual up on the company's intranet, he knows that the white, monolingual executive who runs operations may turn out to be an excellent advocate.

Of course, tempered radicals know that not everyone is an ally, but they also know it's pointless to see those who represent the status quo as enemies. The senior women found fault with an inequitable evaluation system, not with their male colleagues. Paul won David's help by giving him the benefit of the doubt from the very beginning of their relationship. Indeed, tempered radicals constantly consider all possible courses of action: "Under what conditions, for what issues, and in what circumstances does it make sense to join forces with others?"; "How can I best use this alliance to support my efforts?"

Tempered radicals bear no banners; they sound no trumpets. Their ends are sweeping, but their means are mundane.

CLEARLY, THERE IS NO ONE RIGHT WAY to effect change. What works for one individual under one set of circumstances may not work for others under different conditions. The examples above illustrate how tempered radicals use a spectrum of quiet approaches to change their organizations. Some actions are small, private, and muted; some are larger and more public. Their influence spreads as they recruit others and spawn conversations. Top managers can learn a lot from these people about the mechanics of evolutionary change.

Tempered radicals bear no banners; they sound no trumpets. Their ends are sweeping, but their means are mundane. They are firm in their commitments, yet flexible in the ways they fulfill them. Their actions may be small but can spread like a virus. They yearn for rapid change but trust in patience. They often work individually yet pull people together. Instead of stridently pressing their agendas, they start conversations. Rather than battling powerful foes, they seek powerful friends. And in the face of setbacks, they keep going. To do all this, tempered radicals understand revolutionary change for what it is—a phenomenon that can occur suddenly but more often than not requires time, commitment, and the patience to endure.

How the Research Was Done

THIS ARTICLE IS BASED ON a multipart research effort that I began in 1986 with Maureen Scully, a professor of management at the Center for Gender in Organizations at Simmons Graduate School of Management in Boston. We had observed a number of people in our own occupation—academia—who, for various reasons, felt at odds with the prevailing culture of their institutions. Initially, we set out to understand how these individuals sustained their sense of self amid pressure to conform and how they managed to uphold their values without jeopardizing their careers. Eventually, this research broadened to include interviews with individuals in a variety of organizations and occupations: business people, doctors, nurses, lawyers, architects, administrators, and engineers at various levels of seniority in their organizations.

Since 1986, I have observed and interviewed dozens of tempered radicals in many occupations and conducted focused research with 236 men and women, ranging from mid-level professionals to CEOs. The sample was diverse, including people of different races, nationalities, ages, religions, and sexual orientations, and people who hold a wide range of values and change agendas. Most of these people worked in one of three publicly traded corporations—a financial services organization, a high-growth computer components corporation, and a company that makes and sells consumer products. In this portion of the research, I set out to learn more about the challenges tempered radicals face and discover their strategies for surviving, thriving, and fomenting change. The sum of this research resulted in the spectrum of strategies described in this article.

Tempered Radicals as Everyday Leaders

IN THE COURSE OF THEIR daily actions and interactions, tempered radicals teach important lessons and inspire change. In so doing, they exercise a form of leadership within organizations that is less visible than traditional forms—but just as important.

The trick for organizations is to locate and nurture this subtle form of leadership. Consider how Barry Coswell, a conservative, yet open-minded lawyer who headed up the securities division of a large, distinguished financial services firm, identified, protected, and promoted a tempered radical within his organization. Dana, a left-of-center, first-year attorney, came to his office on her first day of work after having been fingerprinted—a standard

practice in the securities industry. The procedure had
made Dana nervous: What would happen when her
new employer discovered that she had done jail time for
participating in a 1960s-era civil rights protest? Dana
quickly understood that her only hope of survival was to
be honest about her background and principles. Despite
the difference in their political proclivities, she decided to
give Barry the benefit of the doubt. She marched into his
office and confessed to having gone to jail for sitting in
front of a bus.

"I appreciate your honesty," Barry laughed, "but
unless you've broken a securities law, you're probably
okay." In return for her small confidence, Barry shared
stories of his own about growing up in a poor county
and about his life in the military. The story swapping
allowed them to put aside ideological disagreements
and to develop a deep respect for each other. Barry
sensed a budding leader in Dana. Here was a woman
who operated on the strength of her convictions and
was honest about it but was capable of discussing her
beliefs without self-righteousness. She didn't pound
tables. She was a good conversationalist. She listened
attentively. And she was able to elicit surprising confes-
sions from him.

Barry began to accord Dana a level of protection,
and he encouraged her to speak her mind, take risks,
and most important, challenge his assumptions. In one
instance, Dana spoke up to defend a female junior
lawyer who was being evaluated harshly and, Dana
believed, inequitably. Dana observed that different standards were being applied to male and female lawyers,
but her colleagues dismissed her "liberal" concerns.
Barry cast a glance at Dana, then said to the staff, "Let's
look at this and see if we are being too quick to judge."

After the meeting, Barry and Dana held a conversation about double standards and the pervasiveness of bias. In time, Barry initiated a policy to seek out minority legal counsel, both in-house and at outside legal firms. And Dana became a senior vice president.

In Barry's ability to recognize, mentor, and promote Dana there is a key lesson for executives who are anxious to foster leadership in their organizations. It suggests that leadership development may not rest with expensive external programs or even with the best intentions of the human resources department. Rather it may rest with the open-minded recognition that those who appear to rock the boat may turn out to be the most effective of captains.

Notes

1. With the exception of those in the VA hospital and Allied Domecq cases, all the names used through this article are fictitious.

Originally published in October 2001
Reprint R0109F

Why Good Companies Go Bad

DONALD N. SULL

Executive Summary

ONE OF THE MOST COMMON business phenomena
is also one of the most perplexing: when successful companies face big changes, they often fail to respond effectively. Many assume that the problem is paralysis, but the
real problem, according to Donald Sull, is *active inertia*—
an organization's tendency to persist in established patterns of behavior.

Most leading businesses owe their prosperity to a
fresh competitive formula—a distinctive combination of
strategies, relationships, processes, and values that sets
them apart from the crowd. But when changes occur in a
company's markets, the formula that brought success
instead brings failure. Stuck in the modes of thinking and
working that have been successful in the past, market
leaders simply accelerate all their tried-and-true activities.
In attempting to dig themselves out of a hole, they just
deepen it.

83

In particular, four things happen: strategic frames become blinders; processes harden into routines; relationships become shackles; and values turn into dogmas. To illustrate his point, the author draws on examples of pairs of industry leaders, like Goodyear and Firestone, whose fates diverged when they were forced to respond to dramatic changes in the tire industry.

In addition to diagnosing the problem, Sull offers practical advice for avoiding active inertia. Rather than rushing to ask, "What should we do?" managers should pause to ask, "What hinders us?" That question focuses attention on the proper things: the strategic frames, processes, relationships, and values that can subvert action by channeling it in the wrong direction.

ONE OF THE MOST COMMON business phenomena is also one of the most perplexing: when successful companies face big changes in their environment, they often fail to respond effectively. Unable to defend themselves against competitors armed with new products, technologies, or strategies, they watch their sales and profits erode, their best people leave, and their stock valuations tumble. Some ultimately manage to recover—usually after painful rounds of downsizing and restructuring— but many don't.

Why do good companies go bad? It's often assumed that the problem is paralysis. Confronted with a disruption in business conditions, companies freeze; they're caught like the proverbial deer in the headlights. But that explanation doesn't fit the facts. In studying once-thriving companies that have struggled in the face of change, I've found little evidence of paralysis. Quite the contrary. The managers of besieged companies usually recognize the threat early, carefully analyze its implications for their business, and unleash a flurry of initiatives in response. For all the activity, though, the companies still falter.

The problem is not an inability to take action but an inability to take appropriate action. There can be many reasons for the problem—ranging from managerial stubbornness to sheer incompetence—but one of the most common is a condition that I call *active inertia*. Inertia is usually associated with inaction—picture a billiard ball at rest on a table—but physicists also use the term to describe a moving object's tendency to persist in its current trajectory. Active inertia is an organization's tendency to follow established patterns of behavior—even in response to dramatic environmental shifts. Stuck in the modes of thinking and working that brought success in the past, market leaders simply accelerate all their tried-and-true activities. In trying to dig themselves out of a hole, they just deepen it.

Because active inertia is so common, it's important to understand its sources and symptoms. After all, if executives assume that the enemy is paralysis, they will automatically conclude that the best defense is action. But if they see that action itself can be the enemy, they will look more deeply into all their assumptions before acting. They will, as a result, gain a clearer view of what really needs to be done and, equally important, what may prevent them from doing it. And they will significantly reduce the odds of joining the ranks of fallen leaders. (See "Are You Suffering from Active Inertia" at the end of this article.)

Victims of Active Inertia

To see the destructive potential of active inertia, consider the examples of Firestone Tire & Rubber and Laura
Ashley. Both companies were leading players in their
industries, and both failed to meet the challenge of
change—not because they didn't act but because they
didn't act appropriately.

As Firestone entered the 1970s, it was enjoying seven
decades of uninterrupted growth. It sat atop the thriving
U.S. tire industry, alongside Goodyear, its crosstown rival
in Akron, Ohio. Firestone's managers had a clear vision
of their company's positioning and strategy. They saw
the Big Three Detroit automakers as their key customers,
they saw Goodyear and the other leading U.S. tire makers
as their competitors, and they saw their challenge as
simply keeping up with the steadily increasing demand
for tires.

The company had become a monument to its own
success. Its culture and operations reflected the vision of
its founder, Harvey Firestone, Sr., who insisted on treating customers and employees as part of the "Firestone
family." The Firestone country club was open to all
employees, regardless of rank, and Harvey himself maintained close friendships with the top executives of the
big carmakers. (In fact, his granddaughter married Henry
Ford's grandson.) Firestone created fiercely loyal managers, steeping them in the company's family values and
in its Akron-centered worldview.

The company's operating and capital allocation processes were designed to exploit the booming demand for
tires by quickly bringing new production capacity on
line. In the capital-budgeting process, for example, frontline employees identified market opportunities and

translated them into proposals for investing in additional capacity. Middle managers then selected the most promising proposals and presented them to top executives, who tended to speedily approve the middle managers' recommendations.

Firestone's long-standing success gave the company a strong, unified sense of its strategies and values, its relationships with customers and employees, and its operating and investment processes. The company had, in short, a clear formula for success, which had served it well since the turn of the century.

Then, almost overnight, everything changed. A French company, Michelin, introduced the radial tire to the U.S. market. Based on a breakthrough in design, radials were safer, longer-lasting, and more economical than traditional bias tires. They had already come to dominate European markets, and when Ford declared in 1972 that all its new cars would have radials, it was clear that they would dominate the U.S. market, too.

Firestone was not taken by surprise by the arrival of radials. Through its large operations in Europe, it had witnessed firsthand the European markets' quick embrace of radial tires during the 1960s. And it had developed forecasts that clearly indicated that radials would be rapidly accepted by U.S. automakers and consumers as well. Firestone saw radials coming, and it swiftly took action: it invested nearly $400 million—more than $1 billion in today's dollars—in radial production, building a new plant dedicated to radial tires and converting several existing factories.

Although Firestone's response was quick, it was far from effective. Even as it invested in the new product, it clung to its old ways of working. Rather than redesign its production processes, it just tinkered with them—even

though the manufacture of radial tires required much
higher quality standards. In addition, the company
delayed closing many of its factories that produced bias
tires, despite clearindications of their impending obso-
lescence. Active inertia had taken hold.

By 1979, Firestone was in deep trouble. Its plants were
running at an anemic 59% of capacity, it was renting
warehouses to store unsold tires, it was plagued by costly
and embarrassing product recalls, and its domestic tire
business had burned more than $200 million in cash.
Although overall U.S. tire sales were plateauing, largely
because radials last twice as long as bias tires, Firestone's
CEO clung to the assumption of ever-growing demand,
telling the board that he saw no need to start closing
plants. In the end, all of Firestone's intense analysis and
action was for naught. The company surrendered much
of its share of the U.S. market to foreign corporations,
and it suffered through two hostile takeover bids before
finally being acquired by Bridgestone, a Japanese company, in 1988.

The women's apparel maker Laura Ashley also fell vic-
tim to active inertia. The company's eponymous founder
spent her youth in Wales, and she started the business
with her husband, Bernard, in 1953 as a way to re-create
the mood of the British countryside. The company's garments, designed to evoke a romantic vision of English
ladies tending roses at their country manors, struck a
chord with many women in the 1970s. The business grew
quickly from a single silk-screen press in Laura and
Bernard's London flat to a major retailer with a network
of 500 shops and a powerful brand the world over.

Laura Ashley expanded her tiny operation not to
maximize profits but to defend and promote traditional
British values, which she felt were under siege from sex,

drugs, and miniskirts in the 1960s. From the beginning, she and Bernard exercised tight control over all aspects of the business, keeping design, manufacturing, distribution, and retailing in-house. The couple opened a central manufacturing and distribution center in Wales, and they proudly labeled their garments "Made in Wales." They provided generous wages and benefits to their employees, thereby avoiding the labor unrest that crippled many British industries throughout the 1970s. They also established close relationships with their franchisees and customers, who grew fiercely loyal to the company's products and the values they embodied.

When Laura died in 1985, Bernard kept the company on the course his wife had set. Fashion, however, changed. As more women entered the workforce, they increasingly chose practical, professional attire over Laura Ashley's romantic garb. Competitors publicly dismissed the Laura Ashley style as better suited to milkmaids in the 1880s than CEOs in the 1980s. At the same time, apparel manufacturing was undergoing a transformation. With trade barriers falling, fashion houses were rushing to move production offshore or to outsource it entirely, dramatically reducing their operating costs. Laura Ashley, in contrast, continued to pursue the outdated designs and the expensive manufacturing processes that had served it so well in the past.

The company did not, however, suffer from paralysis. By the late 1980s, an outside consultant had identified the major challenges facing Laura Ashley and had outlined remedial actions. Recognizing the need to act, the board of directors, chaired by Bernard, brought in a series of new CEOs, asking each to develop and carry out a restructuring plan that would increase sales and cut costs. The new plans set off flurries of activity, but none of them went far enough in recasting the company's strategy. It remained unclear whether Laura Ashley was a brand, a manufacturer, a retailer, or an integrated fashion company. Nor did the plans refresh the company's traditional values to bring them in line with the marketplace. Afflicted with active inertia, Laura Ashley went through seven CEOs in a decade, but the company's decline continued.

The fresh thinking that led to a company's initial success is often replaced by a rigid devotion to the status quo.

American televangelist Pat Robertson recently joined the board as an outside director, leading one financial journal to conclude that the company sought divine inspiration for its earthly problems.

The Four Hallmarks of Active Inertia

To understand why successful companies like Firestone and Laura Ashley fail, it is necessary to examine the origins of their success. Most leading businesses owe their prosperity to a fresh competitive formula—a distinctive combination of strategies, processes, relationships, and values that sets them apart from the crowd. As the formula succeeds, customers multiply, talented workers flock to apply, investors bid up the stock, and competitors respond with the sincerest form of flattery—imitation. All this positive feedback reinforces managers' confidence that they have found the one best way, and it emboldens them to focus their energies on refining and extending their winning system.

Frequently, though, the system begins to harden. The fresh thinking that led to a company's initial success is replaced by a rigid devotion to the status quo. And when changes occur in the company's markets, the formula that had brought success instead brings failure. (See the exhibit "The Dynamic of Failure.") In particular, four things happen:

Strategic frames become blinders. Strategic frames are the mental models—the mind-sets—that shape how managers see the world. The frames provide the answers to key strategic questions: What business are we in? How do we create value? Who are our competitors? Which customers are crucial, and which can we safely ignore? And they concentrate managers' attention on what is

---

The Dynamic of Failure

Leading companies can become stuck in the modes of thinking and working that brought them their initial success. When business conditions change, their once-winning formulas instead bring failure.

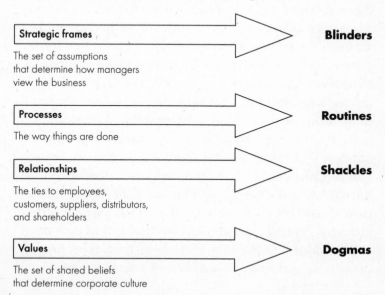

Strategic frames → **Blinders**
The set of assumptions that determine how managers view the business

Processes → **Routines**
The way things are done

Relationships → **Shackles**
The ties to employees, customers, suppliers, distributors, and shareholders

Values → **Dogmas**
The set of shared beliefs that determine corporate culture

important among the jumble of raw data that crosses their desks and computer screens every day. The strategic frames of Firestone's managers, for example, focused their eyes on their competitors around Akron and their customers in Detroit. The frames also help managers see patterns in complex data by fitting the information into an established model. In Laura Ashley's heyday, its strategic frames enabled its executives to quickly judge potential product extensions based on their fit with traditional English style.

But while frames help managers to see, they can also blind them. By focusing managers' attention repeatedly on certain things, frames can seduce them into believing that these are the only things that matter. In effect, frames can constrict peripheral vision, preventing people from noticing new options and opportunities. Although Firestone competed head-to-head with Michelin in Europe and had witnessed the rapid rise of radial tires there, its leaders still couldn't see the French company as a serious competitor in their core domestic market. As a strategic frame grows more rigid, managers often force surprising information into existing schema or ignore it altogether. Laura Ashley's managers repeatedly dismissed sales declines as temporary fluctuations rather than as indicators of basic shifts in women's fashion.

Sadly, the transformation of strategic frames into blinders is the rule, not the exception, in most human affairs. Consider the disastrous evolution of France's military strategy during the first half of this century. At the turn of the century, French military doctrine glorified attack, reflecting a belief that élan vital would prevail over all odds. But the attack-at-all-costs strategy proved disastrous in the trenches of World War I. As a result, the country's military changed its strategic frame and adopted a purely defensive posture, which took concrete form in the Maginot Line, a series of fixed fortifications erected to protect France's borders from German invasion. These fixed defenses, however, proved worthless in halting blitzkrieg attacks. The hard-won lesson from the First World War became a tragic blinder during the Second.

When strategic frames grow rigid, companies, like nations, tend to keep fighting the last war. When Xerox's management surveyed the competitive battlefield in the 1970s, it saw IBM and Kodak as the enemy, its 40,000 sales and service representatives as its troops, and its patented technologies as its insurmountable defenses. Xerox's frames enabled the company to fight off traditional foes using established tactics and to rebuff repeated attempts by IBM and Kodak to attack its core market. But the strategic frames blinded Xerox to the new threat posed by guerrilla warriors such as Canon and Ricoh, which were targeting individuals and small companies for their high-quality compact copiers.

Once Xerox's management recognized the magnitude of the threat from the new entrants, it belatedly but aggressively launched a series of quality programs designed to beat the Japanese at their own game. These initiatives did stem Xerox's share loss, and the company's victory over the Japanese was trumpeted in books with titles like *Xerox: American Samurai*. The focus on beating the Japanese, however, distracted Xerox's management from the emerging battle for the personal computer. At the time, Xerox's Palo Alto Research Center was pioneering several of the technologies that sparked the personal computer revolution,

including the graphical user interface and the mouse.
But Xerox was unable to capitalize on the new opportunities because they lay outside its strategic frames.

Processes harden into routines. When a company
decides to do something new, employees usually try several different ways of carrying out the activity. But once
they have found a way that works particularly well, they
have strong incentives to lock into the chosen process
and stop searching for alternatives. Fixing on a single
process frees people's time and energy for other tasks. It
leads to increased productivity, as employees gain experience performing the process. And it also provides the
operational predictability necessary to coordinate the
activities of a complex organization.

But just as with strategic frames, established processes often take on a life of their own. They cease to
be means to an end and become ends in themselves.
People follow the processes not because they're effective
or efficient but because they're well known and comfortable. They are simply "the way things are done."
Once a process becomes a routine, it prevents employees from considering new ways of working. Alternative
processes never get considered, much less tried. Active
inertia sets in.

At Firestone, the routinization of processes was one
of the major impediments to an effective response to
radial technology. The company ran into manufacturing
and quality problems because it tried to accommodate
radial production by just tweaking its existing processes.
Firestone produced tires that no one wanted because its
capital-budgeting process promoted unnecessary investments in capacity—the capital outlays were driven by
frontline managers who, quite understandably, were not

keen to volunteer their own plants for closure. And it failed to bring in people with fresh viewpoints because its executive recruitment and promotion processes concentrated on building loyalty and instilling a uniform mind-set. Even as the company struggled with change, it continued to hire and promote "people like us." In 1972, all of Firestone's top managers had spent their entire careers with the company, two-thirds had been born and raised in Akron, and one-third had followed in their fathers' footsteps as Firestone executives.

McDonald's is another example of a company whose routines have dulled its response to shifting market conditions. In the early 1990s, the fast-food giant's operations manual comprised 750 pages detailing every aspect of a restaurant's business. For years, the company's relentless focus on standardized processes, all dictated by headquarters, had allowed it to rapidly roll out its winning formula in market after market, ensuring the consistency and efficiency that attracted customers and dismayed rivals.

By the 1990s, however, McDonald's was in a rut. Consumers were looking for different and healthier foods, and competitors such as Burger King and Taco Bell were capitalizing on the shift in taste by launching new menu items. McDonald's, however, was slow to respond to the changes. Its historical strength—a single-minded focus on refining its mass-production processes—turned into a weakness. By requiring menu decisions to pass through headquarters, the company stifled innovation and delayed action. Its central development kitchen, removed from the actual restaurants and their customers, churned out a series of products, such as the McPizza, McLean, and Arch Deluxe, but they all failed to entice diners.

Relationships become shackles. In order to succeed, every company must build strong relationships—with employees, customers, suppliers, lenders, and investors. Laura and Bernard Ashley worked diligently to win the hearts of new customers, franchisees, and investors at every step of their company's expansion. Harvey Firestone, Sr., maintained close friendships with his customers, provided loans out of his own pocket to struggling tire dealers during the Great Depression, and socialized with many of his company's top executives. Firestone and the Ashleys, like many successful executives, wove the warp of economic transactions with the woof of social relationships to strengthen the fabric of their companies.

When conditions shift, however, companies often find that their relationships have turned into shackles, limiting their flexibility and leading them into active inertia. The need to maintain existing relationships with customers can hinder companies in developing new products or focusing on new markets.[1] Kirin Brewery, for example, gained control of a daunting 60% share of the postwar Japanese beer market by building strong relationships with businessmen, many of whom had received the company's lager as part of their rations in the army. In the 1980s, Kirin was reluctant to alienate its core customers by offering the trendy dry beer favored by younger drinkers. Kirin's slow response allowed Asahi Breweries to catch up and then surpass it as the industry leader.

Managers can also find themselves constrained by their relationships with employees, as the saga of Apple Computer vividly illustrates. Apple's vision of technically elegant computers and its freewheeling corporate culture attracted some of the most creative engineers in the

world, who went on to develop a string of smash products including the Apple II, the Macintosh, and the
PowerBook. As computers became commodities, Apple
knew that its continued health depended on its ability to
cut costs and speed up time to market. Imposing the
necessary discipline, however, ran counter to the Apple
culture, and top management found itself frustrated
whenever it tried to exert more control. The engineers
simply refused to change their ways. The relationships
with creative employees that enabled Apple's early
growth ultimately hindered it from responding to environmental changes.

Banc One is another company that was hamstrung by
its relationships with employees—in particular, its managers. Growing from humble beginnings, Banc One
became the most profitable U.S. bank in the early 1990s,
with a market capitalization that topped that of American Express and J.P. Morgan. Its formula for success was
to acquire healthy local banks, retain their incumbent
managers, and grant those managers considerable
autonomy in running their businesses. These "uncommon partnerships," as Banc One dubbed the relationships, motivated the managers to act as entrepreneurs
and respond to local market conditions.

But as consolidation and deregulation changed the
banking industry, Banc One began to struggle. Many of
its best customers were being stolen by aggressive new
competitors like Fidelity Investments, and the high cost
of its decentralized, locally focused operations put it at a
disadvantage to more efficient rivals like First Union and
NationsBank. Banc One was slow to standardize its
products and centralize its back-office operations
because it knew that such moves would curb the autonomy of the local bank managers. It regained its upward

momentum only after its CEO, John B. McCoy, decided to abandon the cherished uncommon partnerships altogether.

Relationships with distributors can also turn into shackles. Dell Computer has surged ahead of rival PC makers by selling directly to customers. Incumbents like Hewlett-Packard and IBM have been slow to copy Dell's model, fearing a backlash from the resellers who currently account for the vast majority of their sales. Airlines like Lufthansa, British Airways, and KLM face a similar dilemma. They've been slow to promote direct sales—over the Internet, for example—because they don't want to antagonize the travel agents they rely on for filling seats.

Values harden into dogmas. A company's values are the set of deeply held beliefs that unify and inspire its people. Values define how employees see both themselves and their employers. The "Firestone man," for example, exemplified loyalty to the company and a deep commitment to the community. Values also provide the centripetal force that holds together a company's far-flung operations. Laura Ashley franchisees rallied around the banner of the company's traditional values, helping to create a strong brand identity around the world.

As companies mature, however, their values often harden into rigid rules and regulations that have legitimacy simply because they're enshrined in precedent. Like a petrifying tree, the once-living values are slowly replaced by the cold stone of dogma. As this happens, the values no longer inspire, and their unifying power degenerates into a reactionary tendency to circle the wagons in the face of threats. The result, again, is active inertia.

Polaroid's steady decline illustrates how once-vibrant values can ossify. Founded by inventor Edwin Land, Polaroid rose to prominence by pioneering a series of exciting technologies like instant photography, and its employees prided themselves on the company's R&D leadership. But over time, Polaroid's devotion to excellent research turned into a disdain for other business activities. Marketing and finance, in particular, were considered relatively unimportant so long as the company had cutting-edge technology. Valuing technological breakthroughs above all else, Polaroid's managers continued to invest heavily in research without adequately considering how customers would respond. Not surprisingly, sales stagnated. Today the company is worth only one-third of what a bidder offered in an acquisition attempt in 1989.

Royal Dutch/Shell is another company whose values became a hindrance. During the 1930s, Shell was dominated by Henri Deterding, who was a strong leader and a Nazi sympathizer. Shell's other executives finally forced Deterding out, and the painful episode imprinted on the company a distaste for central control—a value that came to permeate its culture and led to the establishment of fiercely independent country managers. The decentralized structure enabled Shell to seize growth opportunities around the world. But when oil prices fell during the 1990s, the belief in decentralized authority prevented the company from quickly rationalizing its operations and cutting costs.

Renewal, Not Revolution

Success breeds active inertia, and active inertia breeds failure. But is failure an inevitable consequence of success? In business, at least, the answer is no. While Firestone floundered, Goodyear made a smooth transition to radial tires, emerging as one of the three global powers in the tire industry. While Laura Ashley continued its downward drift, Gucci righted itself after a brief stumble. History reveals many such pairs of industry leaders whose fates diverged when they were forced to respond to environmental changes. Think of General Electric and Westinghouse, Volkswagen and Renault, Samsung and the Hanjin Group, Southwest Airlines and People Express.

Successful companies can avoid—or at least overcome—active inertia. First, though, they have to break free from the assumption that their worst enemy is paralysis. They need to realize that action alone solves nothing. In fact, it often makes matters worse. Instead of rushing to ask, "What should we do?" managers should pause to ask, "What hinders us?" That question focuses attention on the proper things: the strategic frames, processes, relationships, and values that can subvert action by channeling it in the wrong direction.

Most struggling companies have a good sense of what they need to do. They have stacks of reports from inside analysts and outside consultants, all filled with the same kinds of recommendations. Firestone's leaders were well aware of the superiority of the radial tire, and Laura Ashley's executives knew that more and more women were joining the workforce. Their problem was that they lacked a clear understanding of how their old formulas for success would hinder them in responding to the changes.

Even after a company has come to understand the obstacles it faces, it should resist the impulse to rush forward. Some business gurus exhort managers to change every aspect of their companies simultaneously, to foment revolution within their organizations. The assumption is that the old formulas need to be thrown to the wind—and the sooner, the better. But the veterans of change programs whom I've talked to argue against that approach. They say that by trying to change everything all at once, managers often destroy crucial competencies, tear the fabric of social relationships that took years to weave, and disorient customers and employees alike. A revolution provides a shock to the system, but the shock sometimes proves fatal.

Look at what happened when Firestone finally recognized the obstacles that were preventing it from succeeding. In 1980, Firestone's board brought in a CEO known for his prowess as a turnaround artist. The new chief executive wasted no time. He closed five of the company's 14 domestic plants, severed its long-standing relationships with several customers, replaced the bottom-up capital-budgeting process with a strict top-down approach, and filled key management posts with a crew of outsiders. (See "The Inside-Outsider as Change Leader" at the end of this article.)

The new CEO's revolution saved Firestone from bankruptcy, but it left the company poorly positioned for future growth. The team of outside managers disposed of several of Firestone's most promising businesses and invested heavily in tire retailing, despite warnings from seasoned insiders that the company's tire stores had never been profitable. Firestone's days as an independent company were numbered.

Goodyear, by contrast, took a very different path. Respectful of its corporate heritage but not beholden to it, Goodyear adapted to the new competitive environment through a series of carefully staged changes,

avoiding the need for a revolution. The company cut its
production capacity for traditional tires in a way that
showed respect for its long standing commitments to
workers and communities. Wherever possible, it converted existing factories to radial production or built
new radial facilities adjacent to closed plants, retaining
most employees and thus mitigating the disruption to
the communities. And whereas Firestone radically
reduced its level of customer service, Goodyear continued to invest in its customer relationships, establishing a
basis for future growth.

If ever there appeared to be a candidate for revolution
it was IBM in 1993. When Lou Gerstner left RJR Nabisco
to take the helm at IBM, he entered a company that had
lost more than $16 billion in three years, had been sin-
gled out as a dinosaur by *Fortune*, and was in the process
of being carved into 13 divisions that could be sold off in
chunks. Gerstner shook up the hidebound IBM culture
and slashed costs, but he also preserved and nurtured
many of IBM's traditional strengths. Rather than ape the
freewheeling style of Silicon Valley companies, Gerstner
emphasized IBM's reputation for stability and responsibility. He reassured corporate customers that they could
rely on Big Blue to help them move into the world of net-
worked computers. Instead of abandoning IBM's main-
frame business, Gerstner expanded services and
acquired software that complemented IBM's heavy
metal, enabling the company to offer "total solutions" to
customers' information technology needs. Gerstner's
strategy of transforming IBM through renewal rather
than revolution has succeeded beyond anyone's expectations, leading to a more than fourfold increase in the
company's share price and positioning it to continue as
an industry leader into the next century.

IBM's turnaround offers an important lesson to any successful company facing big changes. Active inertia exists because the pull of the past is so strong. Trying to break that pull through a radical act of organizational revolution leaves people disoriented and disenfranchised, cut off from the past but unprepared to enter the future. It's better for managers to respect the company's heritage. They should build on the foundations of the past even as they teach employees that old strategic frames, processes, relationships, and values need to be recast to meet new challenges.

Are You Suffering from Active Inertia?

ACTIVE INERTIA IS INSIDIOUS BY NATURE. Because it grows out of success, it often spreads unnoticed in corporations. Sometimes, in fact, what managers consider to be their company's strengths are actually signs of weakness. If many of the following statements ring true for your company, you may want to take a fresh look at your strategic frames, processes, relationships, and values.

"We know our competitors inside out."

"Our top priority is keeping our existing customers happy."

"We're not the world's greatest innovators, but we run a tight ship."

"Our processes are so well tuned that the company could practically run itself."

"We focus R&D on product refinements and extensions, not on product breakthroughs."

"We're skeptics. In our view, the leading edge is the bleeding edge."

"We can't allow ourselves to get distracted by all the new fads in the marketplace."

"We have a very stable top-management team."

"We have a well-entrenched corporate culture."

"We will never relinquish our core competency."

"Our processes are world class, and we follow them religiously."

"If it ain't broke, we don't fix it."

"We have high levels of employee loyalty, but when we bring in talented new people, they often get frustrated and leave."

"We've carved out an enduring leadership position in our industry."

"We view our current distributors as key strategic partners. We don't want to alienate them by rushing into new channels."

"Our corporate values are sacred; we'll never change them."

The Inside-Outsider as Change Leader

GUIDING A COMPANY THROUGH big changes requires a difficult balancing act. The company's heritage has to be respected even as it's being resisted. It's often assumed that outside managers are best suited to lead such an effort, since they're not bound by the company's historical formula. Lou Gerstner's success in turning IBM around is frequently held up as evidence of the need for an outsider. I would argue, though, that Gerstner should be viewed more as an exception than an example. Typically, outsiders are so quick to throw out all the old ways of working that they end up doing more harm than good.

The approach I recommend is to look for new leaders from within the company but from outside the core business. These managers, whom I call inside-outsiders, can be drawn from the company's smaller divisions, from international operations, or from staff functions. Charles Pilliod, for example, the CEO who led Goodyear into the radial age, was born and raised in Akron and worked his entire career with Goodyear. But he had spent 29 of his 31 years prior to taking the helm at Goodyear in the company's international division, where he had watched the rapid spread of radials in Europe. He understood the company's heritage, but he could see it from the objective viewpoint of an outsider.

Inside-outsiders have led many of the most dramatic corporate transformations in recent times: Jack Welch spent most of his career in GE's plastics business; Jürgen Schrempp was posted in South Africa before returning to run Daimler-Benz, now Daimler Chrysler; and Domenico De Sole served as the Gucci Group's legal counsel before leading that company's dramatic rejuvenation.

Another alternative is to assemble management teams that leverage the strengths of both insiders and outsiders. When Gerstner took over at IBM, he didn't force out all the old guard. Most operating positions continued to be staffed by IBM veterans with decades of experience, but they were supported by outsiders in key staff slots and marketing roles. The combination of perspectives has allowed IBM to use old strengths to fuel its passage down an entirely new course.

Finally, inside managers can break free of their old formulas by imagining themselves as outsiders, as Intel's executives did in deciding to abandon the memory business. Intel had pioneered the market for memory chips, and for most of its executives, employees, and customers, Intel meant memory. As new competitors entered the market, however, Intel saw its share of the memory business dwindle from more than 90% in the early 1970s to about 5% a decade later. At the same time, increasing industry capacity was stifling prices.

Although Intel had built an attractive microprocessor business during this time, it clung to the memory business until its chairman, Gordon Moore, and its president, Andy Grove, sat down and deliberately imagined what would happen if they were replaced with outsiders. They agreed that outsiders would get out of the memory business—and that's exactly what Moore and Grove did. While a company's competitive formula exerts a tremendous gravitational pull, thinking like outsiders can help insiders to break free.

Notes

1. For a discussion of how relationships with customers can prevent a company from innovating, see Joseph L. Bower and Clayton M. Christensen, "Disruptive Technologies: Catching the Wave," HBR January–February 1995.

Originally published in July–August 1999
Reprint 99410

Transforming a Conservative Company—One Laugh at a Time

KATHERINE M. HUDSON

Executive Summary

YOU WOULDN'T THINK OF Brady Corporation as an obvious place in which to find a fun culture. This traditional Midwestern company, a manufacturer of industrial signs and other identification products, didn't even allow employees to have coffee at their desks until 1989. But when Katherine Hudson became CEO in 1994, she and her executive team determined that injecting some fun into the company's serious culture could create positive effects within the organization and contribute to increased performance and sales.

In this article, Hudson distills her approach to overhauling Brady's culture into six principles of serious fun: More people than you might think are comfortable having fun at work; used with an awareness of cultural sensitivities, fun and laughter really are well-understood international languages; humor can help companies get through tough times; fun can be embodied in formal programs; spontaneous efforts at humor can also be effective; and encouraging fun should begin at the top. She richly illustrates each principle with examples.

At Brady, getting people to loosen up and enjoy themselves has fostered a company esprit de corps and greater team camaraderie. It has started conversations that have sparked innovation, helped to memorably convey corporate messages to employees, and increased productivity by reducing stress, among other benefits. And the company has doubled its sales and almost tripled its net income and market capitalization over the past seven years. Brady's experience suggests that promoting fun within the workplace can lead not only to a robust corporate culture but also to improved business performance.

W E'RE A COMPANY—maybe like yours—where having fun was long viewed with suspicion. Sure, a lot of start-ups and Silicon Valley companies have wild and crazy cultures, with pillow fights around the foosball table the order of the day. But ours is a traditional, Midwestern manufacturing company, one that didn't even allow employees to have coffee at their desks until 1989. Although we pride ourselves on our technological innovation, we make industrial signs and other identification products, not PalmPilots or rainbow-colored iMacs. We are an old-line company that has always taken business very seriously—again, maybe like yours.

So perhaps it comes as a surprise that, for the past seven years, we've made fun an integral part of the culture at Brady Corporation—not simply as an end in itself but for serious business reasons. We've found that getting people to loosen up and enjoy themselves has numerous benefits. It can break down jealously guarded turf boundaries. It can foster an esprit de corps throughout the company and greater camaraderie on teams. It can start the conversations that spark innovation and increase the likelihood that unpleasant tasks will be accomplished. It can help convey important corporate messages to employees in memorable ways. It can relieve stress—and, heaven knows, we can all benefit from that.

Now, let's be honest: Not everyone at Brady walks around wearing a grin. In fact, I am certain that more than a few employees feel Brady is anything but a fun place to work. I also want to make a confession: Occasionally I wonder if, in making the case for fun, I'm simply seeking a business rationale for having a good laugh—something I definitely like to do, on the job and off! After all, life is short.

In the end, though, I think injecting a dose of fun into a corporate culture represents something much more significant. Certainly, it must be done with care. And it can't be forced. But in the right spirit, selective—or even random—acts of fun can help transform an organization. Let me tell you how we did it at our company.

An Uptight and Cautious Culture

Don't let me mislead you about Brady. Despite its quite conservative culture, the Milwaukee-based company has never been provincial or hidebound in its business outlook. Our 3,200 employees work in more than 20 countries and serve customers in more than 70. We sell 50,000 products, ranging from OSHA-mandated workplace signs to sophisticated labeling software. Last year, we earned nearly $50 million on revenue of about $550 million. The total return to shareholders has grown an average of more than 16% per year since the company went public in 1984. Our shares are listed on the New York Stock Exchange.

Furthermore, the company, founded in 1914 as a maker of advertising calendars and tin roadside signs, has always had a strong entrepreneurial tradition. William H. Brady, Jr., who was CEO for more than 30 years, identified promising executives and then encouraged them to identify promising business opportunities. Legend has it that if you had an idea and could grow it into a $10 million operation, you got a company car and a building for your business.

But over time, this entrepreneurial approach resulted in a company with a lot of small niche enterprises, each a fiefdom protective of its territory and reluctant to cooperate with others. In addition, the culture was patriarchal and conservative. Bill Brady was a larger-than-life figure who kept an eagle eye on company finances. Stories abound of his frugal ways: splitting the check for a business lunch at the local bowling alley, establishing a fiscal year ending on July 31 because hiring auditors costs less at that time of year. Brady's strong hand and fiscal conservatism meant that asking for permission to act rather than taking the initiative on the job was the norm for employees. It's true that coffee was not allowed at employees' desks until—and people know the exact date—August 1, 1989.

Upon taking over as CEO in 1994, I spent my first 90 days visiting all the offices and the manufacturing plants around the world to meet as many employees as possible. Although I know I missed some third-shift folks in manufacturing, I probably shook hands with 80% of the workforce. Now it's true that the people I met during those visits were justifiably guarded as they greeted an unknown CEO, the first to come from outside the company. Just the same, my overriding impression—despite some important cultural changes initiated by two CEOs who had succeeded Bill Brady after he stepped down in 1986—was that Brady people seemed unusually uptight and cautious.

For example, in Canada, I found that the local managers of two Brady units—Seton, a catalog business that sells signs directly to customers, and Signmark, which sells signs through distributors—barely talked to one another. Fifteen years after Brady had acquired Seton, the channel conflict with Signmark still generated immense ill will. The cautious side of the culture became clear to me on a trip to Asia. Brady's manager in Hong Kong hesitantly asked me if he might hire another half a salesperson. His jaw dropped when I suggested that he hire five, if he could give me a commercial justification.

Our problems may have been somewhat extreme, but most managers will recognize a reluctance to collaborate or a fear of risk taking among their own employees. It's what I call a "culture of no." And yet, we had so much potential. Brady was, in my view, a company waiting to happen. The question was how to get people to say yes to change, to information sharing, to cooperation—or, in the words of our official corporate cheer, to go "from no to yo."

Having fun wasn't the core idea. Basically, I wanted to promote an open, collaborative, and trusting can-do atmosphere. For example, we instituted flextime and eliminated time cards for our manufacturing workers.

Although they still earn overtime pay, our blue-collar
workers are treated like salaried employees: We expect
them to be here and do their jobs without managers
looking over their shoulders. When employees need to
juggle their schedules, they work it out with members of
their team and their team leader.

And we emphasize honesty. This means being open
with our customers, our communities (we were ranked
number 27 on *Business Ethics* magazine's 2001 list of the
100 best corporate citizens), and with one another. We
want employees to feel free to acknowledge mistakes and
to share them with colleagues, who in turn are expected
to be supportive and to help turn missteps into learning
experiences.

But I've also found that, if you want people to "just say
yo," it doesn't hurt to bring some fun and humor to the
work environment. Receiving a yo-yo—a "Double Yo
Award"—isn't much of a financial incentive to change
behavior. But it does help imprint in people's minds the
spirit we're trying to encourage at Brady.

Six Principles of Serious Fun

Clearly, you can't get away with promoting a fun culture
unless you show hard business results. And playing or
partying all the time can distract you from achieving
those results. Another risk in trying to bring some levity
to corporate culture: People may find such efforts threat-
ening, offensive, or just plain silly.

But, done deftly, engendering a fun work environment
can contribute to both business performance and a
robust corporate culture. (For three examples of how
Brady has benefited from not taking itself too seriously,
see "Doing the Packarena," "From No to Yo," and "When

the Camel Died" at the end of this article.) A few simple principles can help you to succeed.

People aren't always as stiff as they seem. Some people will undoubtedly object to attempts to bring a bit of levity into the workplace. They may find it inappropriate for a place of business. If the boss is organizing a "fun" activity, they may find it patronizing. Or they may simply feel uncomfortable participating. Let's face it, some people just don't like to yuk it up. And that's okay, as long as their point of view is respected and they feel safe expressing it.

At the same time, however, I find that many people are more comfortable having fun at work than you—or they—initially think, especially when they know that fun is an accepted part of the culture. For example, early on in my tenure, we decided to significantly change Brady's organizational structure by creating the position of global business unit manager. Our CFO at the time was of Italian descent, and he jokingly shortened the term global business unit manager to "gumba"—Italian-American slang for a regular guy.

After we decided to reorganize, one of my most buttoned-down managers requested a meeting with me on short notice. He was one of my best people, and I was thinking, "Oh gosh, he's going to tell me he's leaving." Well, he came into my office, sat down, and said very soberly: "I want to be a gumba." I was shocked until I realized that the manager, whom I viewed as completely serious, was playfully jerking my chain.

Laughter is an international language. People often say that humor doesn't translate well, but I think that a spirit of fun can indeed be transmitted across national

boundaries. For example, when we doubled the size of
our manufacturing plant in Brazil, I went there to cut the
ribbon. I gave my speech in very rough Portuguese and,
at the end, the workers gave a shout in unison. It took
me a split second to realize what they were saying: "Yo!"

When I was at Kodak, I had a meeting with some
managers in Germany. Several days before, I'd been
quoted in a U.S. business magazine on the topic of cultural differences. I said I'd feel comfortable taking off my
shoes in Japan, where it was a custom, but would never
do it in Germany. Well, you can guess the punch line of
this story. At some point during the meeting, I glanced
under the table and saw that everyone was barefoot—
and soon roaring with laughter.

Clearly, you need to be alert to cultural sensitivities.
But while some delicacy may be required in exporting
the particular sense of humor and fun that exists in the
United States to divisions around the world, I believe the
risks are less than most people imagine.

You can still cut up during tough times. There are
certainly periods at a company when merrymaking is
inappropriate. Two years ago we canceled the annual
company picnic—an elaborate and much anticipated
event called Bradyfest—shortly after we had announced
a significant round of layoffs. Clearly, it wouldn't have
been right to celebrate when people had just lost their
jobs. Canceling the picnic was a way of showing respect
for those who had to leave the company.

At the same time, humor and fun can sometimes help
a company ride out rough times. When I was head of the
instant photography division at Kodak, we effectively
received our death sentence when a court ruled favorably
for Polaroid in a patent case. So we sought ways to keep
up employee morale as we were forced to wind down a

business that we'd finally succeeded in making profitable. At a luncheon of about 50 key people, one of my managers gave me his old pair of air force combat boots as a symbol of the daunting leadership challenge I faced. People had placed bets on whether I'd don the boots on the spot (I did), and those boots became an icon of the division's grittiness in this dire time. Later, we made a videotape for the field sales force to answer their questions and keep up their spirits. It was a standard talking-head video, with me updating people on legal developments and issues such as future customer service. At the conclusion, I turned and walked away, and the camera panned down to my feet, shod in the combat boots. It was gallows humor, but it helped keep people going.

Fun can be institutionalized. Every spring, we ask employees to undertake a major cleanup of their work areas. We have open offices at our corporate headquarters in Milwaukee, so it's important that everyone's spaces be presentable when clients visit. On the factory floor, although work areas are usually fairly tidy for safety reasons, clutter can sometimes creep in. But no one likes this annual rite. So in an effort to infuse a potentially dreary task with a sense of play, we give an annual award—the Brady Housekeeping Seal of Approval—to people with particularly neat work areas. On the appointed day, in the best Martha Stewart getup I can muster, I make the rounds and pass out the prizes. Corny? Maybe. A waste of my time? I don't think so. Besides making a task less onerous for employees, handing out the awards gives me another chance to communicate with them on their turf.

To spark innovation, we established another program and gave it a name: the Lego program, after the little building blocks. On the assumption that a good idea shouldn't have to wait for next year's budget, we initiated off-cycle opportunities to fund promising new ideas. If someone's idea is approved, we award it an actual Lego block, an acknowledgment that the idea represents a building block for Brady's future. In the very first round of candidates, we funded investments in our bar code systems and software and in our catalog company start-ups in Italy and Australia. The businesses that grew out of those ideas account today for more than 10% of the company's annual revenues.

Fun can be ad hoc. If fun can be fostered in formal programs, it can also occur in onetime gags. Brady's vice president of direct marketing, Dick Fisk, is based in Connecticut. Several months ago, he complained that although he likes the hotel where he stays when he's in Milwaukee, the pillows there are terrible: they're foam, and he prefers feathers. So the next time he came to town, the company's top management team presented him with a huge plastic storage container with a down pillow in it. We prominently labeled the container (using, of course, Brady's HandiMark portable sign and label system): "Dick Fisk's Special Pillow." The hotel keeps it for him, and when he checks in, they say, "Oh, Mr. Fisk, we have your pillow for you." It wasn't a big deal, but I like to think that, in a small way, it strengthened our team. (Dick responded to this act of generosity by giving everyone on the team a set of Billy Bob teeth!)

The CEO sets the tone. I try in my own behavior to create an atmosphere of fun. If people see me laughing at myself—if they see that I'm even comfortable with people occasionally getting a laugh at my expense—I think that makes me more approachable and also lets others know that having a good time is okay at Brady.

For example, I try to make my office a fun and wel-
coming place. One of the first things I did when I arrived
at Brady was to find a doorstop for my door. Now my
office is a regular destination on the formal orientation
tour for all new employees. Sometimes I'll return from a
meeting and find 20 people there.

The tour guide will likely be showing everyone a
group portrait of some of Brady's top executives, all of us
wearing Groucho Marx glasses and standing before the
"Great Wall of China"—a sweeping display of mounted
toilets at the Kohler bathroom fixtures design center
near Milwaukee. Or perhaps the group will be examining
the two nearly life-size mannequins, Sven and Eve, in traditional Scandinavian dress; their names are acronyms
for our Shareholder Value Enhancement and Employee
Value Enhancement initiatives. Or they may note the
giant bulletproof yo-yo that a Brady team gave me. I
hope that new employees will see that I don't take myself
too seriously and will feel emboldened to stop in later to
share a suggestion or a concern.

Carrying the Fun Gene

Highlighting the importance of the CEO in creating a fun
corporate culture raises a question: To what degree does
this notion depend on his or her personality? While I
have tried here to tease out some generalizable principles, inauthentic efforts by an executive to artificially
impose fun on a company are likely to land with a thud.

It's true that, in some ways, the culture I have tried to
foster at Brady simply reflects my personal style, which
itself mirrors the fun-loving family in which I grew up.
Both of my parents loved a good laugh. My father was a
middle manager at Kodak—in fact, I had his old office

some years after he died—and he used to have fun with his colleagues and direct reports. The photo of the Brady people wearing Groucho Marx glasses echoes a meeting my father once had with his staff, during which everyone wore Mickey Mouse ears he had asked a colleague to buy at Disneyland. And he once sent out a memo to his team referring to a key passage on a particular page of an IBM computer manual. The page was blank, and the ensuing memos debating its meaning gave him—and, when they realized his prank, the others on the team—a chuckle.

And my mother—well, I hardly know where to begin. When my 13-year-old son was young and wanted a bed-time story, we began telling what we call funny grandma stories. These stories—I think we counted 16 in all—capture her can-do, if slightly madcap, approach to life. One time she jumped on my brother's minibike and roared off like Evel Knievel before slipping into a long skid and dis-appearing under a row of pine trees. Another time she vowed to fix a leaky gutter, couldn't figure out why the caulking gun was jammed, squirted herself in the eye while performing an inspection, tipped over the ladder, and ended up hanging from a basketball hoop until my brother rescued her. And she liked telling these stories as much as the next person.

Some of my family's zaniness certainly rubbed off on me, if I didn't inherit it. At Kodak, I think people got used to my antics. (They simply rolled their eyes when I once dressed up as a ghost while flying to a corporate off-site meeting, to protest having to leave my son on Halloween, one of the most important nights of the year for a four-year-old.) At Brady, I just hope that peo-ple appreciate it. After all, the first license plate on my Dodge Ram pickup read "No2Yo," an advertisement for our corporate culture.

Still, the Brady story is about more than just the efforts of one fun-loving woman to create a lively corporate culture. It's true that, at this point in U.S. business, women CEOs, unusual as they are, may have greater freedom to experiment than men do—although I'd say to my male counterparts who feel bound by preconceptions about a male management style, "Hey, you're the boss. Go for it." Furthermore, if you're trying to get your company to loosen up, it clearly will be easier if you're fairly loose yourself.

But just as I've seen relatively solemn employees adopt a spirit of fun when you wouldn't expect it, so I think that all but the most buttoned-down CEOs can get their company cultures to lighten up while remaining true to their own personalities. And I'd argue the potential payoff makes it worth the effort. Certainly there seems to be little risk.

Despite the laughs we've shared at Brady—or, I would argue, in part because of them—the company has doubled its sales and almost tripled its net income and market capitalization over the last seven years. I wouldn't attribute this performance solely to our having a fun culture—or to my being the CEO. Many people and factors have been responsible for the company's success at revitalizing itself.

But our performance is a sign that a company can be fun and friendly for its employees and fierce with its competitors. In fact, the fun has made us fiercer, by making the organization more flexible and dynamic and our people more creative and enthusiastic. And I hope it has made life more enjoyable for people who work here.

Our Signmark division makes a few humorous signs as well as those grim ones warning people to watch out for flammable liquids and slippery floors. One of these novelty signs reads: "I'm not stressed, I eat pencils for fiber." You might say that, ultimately, we're striving to create a workplace where pencils aren't always disappearing from the storeroom.

Doing the Packarena

IN THE SUMMER OF 1996, the Green Bay Packers were looking forward to a promising season. So for our annual Bradyfest picnic, an executive in our Signmark division decided to put together something that would appeal to Brady's ardent Packers fans. He settled on a routine set to the music of the macarena, the popular dance at the time, but with football movements: you take the snap, you step back, you pass, you receive the ball, you celebrate the touchdown.

A local television station came out and filmed a performance of the Packarena from our front yard here at corporate headquarters. About 300 people from all segments of the company showed up in Packers shirts to perform for the cameras. The Packers cheerleaders came down from Green Bay. Well, as soon as the Packarena aired, our switchboard was jammed: People wanted a copy of the "Packarena Playbook," the instructions to do the dance. Soon thereafter, we went to elementary schools to teach the dance to kids. The Green Bay cheerleaders learned it and did it during halftime at one of the Packers' home games.

It's probably the most publicity Brady has ever received. The Packarena was the talk of Milwaukee for weeks. More important, it was the talk of Brady, generating a good feeling about the company among employees both on the factory floor and in the corporate offices.

From No to Yo

ONE OF THE BIG CHALLENGES facing Brady when I arrived in 1994 was the fragmented nature of the company and the competition among business units. So we gathered 50 of Brady's top people at an off-site meeting at a resort near Milwaukee and talked about how we might bridge gaps between divisions and geographies and about the kind of culture we'd like to have at Brady. At one point during the four-day gathering, someone made a great comment about where the company should be heading, and a guy in the audience named Greg Jehlik shouted out: "Yo!" That was immediately the humorous refrain of the meeting. By the end, we'd laid out in a simple document what we wanted our culture to be. I said it seemed like we were describing a journey from no to yo. And that became our cheer for the meeting and for the company.

Although people held back a bit at this initial meeting, a sense of fun was bubbling just below the surface. For example, a fellow named Dan Page stood up and said that in the six years he'd been at Brady, no one had ever thanked him for his efforts. That night, our training manager manufactured a bunch of buttons that said, "Thank you, Dan Page." The next day, everyone was wearing one and walking up to Dan and saying, "Thank you." It was clear that all the elements of a looser culture were there; we only had to free them up.

About a year later, in an effort to spread this cultural change around the company, we decided to gather together more than just 50 managers. So we planned a meeting for roughly one out of every ten people in the company, some 220 employees from all parts of Brady. We couldn't afford to send this many people to a resort, so I decided we'd meet in a dormitory at the University of Wisconsin-Madison. I got loads of resistance.

There was no parking, so we had to take buses from Milwaukee. And although people had single rooms, they had to share bathrooms down the hall. (This was a particular affront to the 50 executives who'd been at the previous year's meeting, which had been held at the American Club, a resort owned by Kohler, the maker of bathroom fixtures. The private bathrooms there were incredible, roughly the size of conference rooms.) At check-in, we gave everybody a pair of flip-flops, a laundry bag, and a soap-on-a-rope with the Brady logo on it.

Most people say it's the best business meeting they've ever attended. The dorm rooms were so spartan that everyone stayed in the common areas and got to know one another. That broke down a lot of barriers. People attended from around the world, and we'd asked each to bring a song in his or her own language along with printouts with phonetic spellings so that people could sing along. Our manager in Japan sang a serious Japanese song, followed by an impromptu performance of "Good Golly, Miss Molly," which he'd performed when he was in a rock band as a kid. It was tremendously fun. And I think people came away from there feeling like they were part of one Brady team.

When the Camel Died

WE CALL IT THE "DEAD CAMEL VIDEO," and it's become part of Brady lore.

In 1995, we were looking for a way to convey to people a vivid vision of the company's future, one of top-line growth achieved by providing complete solutions to our customers' needs. So we decided to make a video that we hoped would portray this message in a memorable way. The production was done in-house, using employees as actors.

The video begins with a man in a long hooded robe crawling on his hands and knees across the desert. (Needless to say, there was a collective guffaw when employees recognized the actor, whose face was mostly obscured by his garment.) Near death, he comes across a sign saying "water" in Arabic—English subtitles provided the translation—with an arrow pointing toward the source. But the Brady sign has blown down, and the man doesn't know which direction to head. So he feebly picks up his cell phone and holds it near the sign's barcode locator tag. The phone scans the information and connects him via satellite with a Brady customer service representative.

The man explains that his camel collapsed two days ago and that he is about to die of thirst. Within hours, the man is sipping a glass of ice water in a parasol-equipped lawn chair shipped to him in the desert from Seton, Brady's direct marketing arm. He has also been offered a replacement camel and a new sign, including an installation option. The message: Growth opportunities exist in the creation of services that are related to but go beyond Brady's products. The hope: People would internalize the message because they had a laugh while absorbing it.

Because the video generated such a buzz, we made another one 18 months later with the same opening scenario. This time, though, we highlighted some of the existing bottlenecks to providing timely and effective customer service: the credit approval process, the handling of customer returns, and foreign exchange conversion, among others. In this version, when a deliveryman arrives with a bottle of water eight days after the camel driver's telephone call, a skeleton is all that's left to accept delivery. Again, while the presentation was humorous, the message was clear and had impact. The video prompted a major, companywide initiative to improve our business processes.

Originally published in July–August 2001
Reprint R0107B

When Your Culture Needs a Makeover

CAROL LAVIN BERNICK

Executive Summary

IN 1994, THE CONSUMER PRODUCTS company
Alberto-Culver North America faced flattened sales and
the most difficult competitive environment of its history.
President Carol Bernick knew that overcoming these
challenges would require a certain kind of corporate culture—but it wasn't the culture the company had. She
changed that by focusing on four areas.

First, Bernick made culture visible and elevated it to
priority status, often by highlighting desired values and
behaviors that already existed in pockets of the company.
Her annual "state of the company" address stresses that
people must be attuned to business realities and the
drivers of success. Employees now develop statements of
individual economic value describing their contributions to
the company's profitability. The company's ten cultural
imperatives are required knowledge for all.

Second, Bernick and her executive team created the role of growth development leader (GDL). Each mentors about a dozen people. Her frequent meetings with GDLs make them effective agents of change upward and downward. The role is coveted because GDLs have real power to make change; every year they vote on the issues, large and small, they must be addressed by the business as a whole.

Third, the company uses an employee survey to identify areas for improvement and to provide 360-degree feedback to GDLs and top management. And fourth, successes are celebrated constantly—through stock awards for the best GDLs, Business Builders Awards for great innovators, and many other, less formal means.

Since 1994, the company has cut employee turnover in half, seen sales grow 83%, and watched pretax profits rise 336%—indicators of how cultural change is driving business results.

I GOT A PHONE CALL not long ago that made my day. It was from one of our suppliers, stranded by weather in Minneapolis and waiting out the delay at a hotel. "Carol, you've got to hear this," he told me. "I was just talking to a guy who's an executive recruiter. When I mentioned I was from Chicago, he said, 'You know, I used to get half my talent from a place there—a company called Alberto-Culver. But not any more. Lately, people there don't even return my calls.'"

I can't say I pitied that recruiter. After all, he and his ilk had picked off our talent for years. Not so long ago, the turnover rate at Alberto-Culver North America—the oldest part of our business and the part I led—was twice the industry average. We were known as a place where people gained a lot of valuable experience fast, but then, if they were good at what they did, cashed it in for better jobs elsewhere.

And turnover wasn't our only problem. In 1994, when my husband and I took the reins of the business my father and mother had built, we faced flattened sales and slipping margins on our best-known consumer brands (although our Sally Beauty Company's stellar performance was allowing the company to report record results). Retailer consolidation was under way, power retailers were emerging, and our competitive environment was getting tougher than ever before. In short, we were in the midst of the most difficult period in our company's history. And, as I looked around me, I realized that the North American organization was not equal to the challenge.

It wasn't our people who were to blame; Culver employees have always been decent and hardworking. It was our culture. We needed people to have a sense of ownership and urgency around the business, to welcome innovation and take risks. But in the existing culture, people dutifully waited for marching orders and thought of their bosses' needs before their customers'. Through long-standing practice, rooted in good intentions, we had sheltered our people from our detailed operating results and all the business realities that drove them. In doing so, we had denied them the knowledge and perspective that could make them our true partners in growing the business.

This is a story about a significant cultural change.

How Did We Get Here?

I'll never forget the day it became clear to me that we were facing a cultural crisis at Alberto-Culver. In late 1992, our head of human resources had engaged an outside consultancy to survey a random sample of employees in order to gain input for our compensation planning. I told him, "Don't bother. If you want my parents' attention [at the time, my father was CEO and human resources reported to my mother], survey only the people they think are the 100 top performers. Those are the people whose judgment they'll trust." They were also, I thought, the least likely to have an ax to grind with the company.

To get the best of both worlds, the consultant surveyed that group as well as a more general employee group and reported the results in tandem. The satisfaction levels of the two groups differed, of course. But the eye-opener was that neither was very satisfied. Even our best people complained about noncompetitive benefits, opaque policies, and lack of family-friendly policies, to name just a few. I remember that day clearly because in less than an hour, I went from feeling pretty good about our company to feeling despair.

When I think of how far we have come since that day in early 1993, I realize we changed our culture by taking four major steps. First, we made an issue of culture, focusing attention and resources on something we had not previously thought much about. Second, we made fixing our culture a job—actually, about 70 jobs. Third, we fashioned ways to measure our gains on the cultural front and did so obsessively. And fourth, we reinforced our stated values by celebrating everything we wanted to see happen again.

Focusing on Culture

As soon as we heard the dismal news of our employee survey, I knew we needed to make cultural change a priority. I immediately asked for budget and other resources to attack the problem. I had no idea how much it would take, and I had little idea what I would even do—but I named a big sum. I only knew I wanted this problem to be on the radar screen.

Now, understand that at heart, I am a marketer. I began my career in the company in the new product department; Static Guard spray and Mrs. Dash seasonings are two innovations I brought to market. My first thought was that the problem with our culture was, to some extent, a matter of perception. Morale would be higher, I suspected, if we stopped hiding our light under a bushel. We went straight to work finding ways to get the word out about all the things we could feel good about as a company.

Finding positive notes to accentuate wasn't hard at all. We had long been a good company and a solid member of our community. In many ways, Alberto-Culver had been one of this country's success stories. It started in 1955 with a single product—Alberto VO5 Hairdressing—that did $100,000 in sales in its first year, not bad since we were competing with the likes of Procter & Gamble and Gillette.

The company took early advantage of television's broad market reach by sponsoring programs like *What's My Line?* and our brands quickly became familiar household names. Our first offering of shares on the New York Stock Exchange, in 1965, took off fast. My father appeared in *Time* in 1963, and in 1973 my mother was named one of *Fortune*'s most influential businesswomen. I've often thought that those early days must have been like life in the heyday of the dot-coms. Even through the 1980s, we posted sales increases every year, and our share price grew 18-fold.

We knew that plenty of innovation and initiative was occurring in pockets of the company, but we had to find it and call attention to it. We held a celebration in our parking lot when we cut paperwork by 30%. Why there? To accommodate the bonfire, of course. And we made people more aware of the many ways we live our company ethics—from a robust program of charitable giving in which employees often get involved, to a fund for helping employees with unexpected financial problems, to our Jumpstart scholarship program that each year helps a number of employees' children further their education.

All this awareness-raising work was having an impact—morale was on the rise—but I also knew that the problem with our culture wasn't simply a matter of perception. We had some realities to adjust, too. We needed to turn members of our North American group into more committed team players. We had to develop a sense of urgency throughout the company and a real hunger for innovation. And just as important, we had to make working at Alberto-Culver more fun. Only if we could make these changes, I thought—and make them last—could our consumer products businesses begin to thrive.

In 1994, my father handed the day-to-day operating control of the business over to my husband, Howard, who became CEO, and myself. We knew cultural change had to be a priority, and we were now in a position to tackle it.

At the outset, my executives were arguing about logic: "Do we make people happy and then the business gets better; or do we fix the business, which will make the people happier?" It was easy for me to answer this: I firmly believe that people drive everything. As it turned out, we focused on both at once, and it wasn't a trade-off after all.

The key to doing both was to recruit everyone in the battle and get every single person focused on the same goals. After a long history of management's keeping its cards close to the vest, we needed to open up and explain the business to our people. Once the facts were on the table, we would find the people who were excited about responding to the challenges.

To get the process started, I invited every Alberto-Culver North America employee to a "state of the company" address, a two-hour intensive look at where we were and where we wanted to be. It's since become an annual event. As I waited for people to file in to that first one, I scattered pennies around the floor, then sat back and watched. Many people glanced at the floor, but no one bothered to pick up a cent.

I started the meeting with the announcement that we were all there to learn and then posed a softball question to the group: "Can anyone name our best-selling product?" The response came back in a happy roar: "VO5 shampoo!" I followed up with another one: "And how about our profits—where do most of them come from?" The group fell into speculation and confusion, and I left it that way for a moment. Then I spoke again. "Look around you on the floor, and if you spot a penny, pick it up. That penny represents our total profit on a bottle of Alberto VO5 shampoo." I then went on to explain that the chain of beauty supply stores called Sally Beauty—

We wanted to create a new world of in-your-face honesty and shared ownership of results.

which the people in Alberto-Culver North America
sometimes considered our side business—was, in fact,
the powerful, growing, profitable driver of the entire
Alberto-Culver Company and, indeed, was carrying the
rest. The process of turning our employees into businesspeople had begun.

Over time, as people became more attuned to our
business challenges, we also helped them see exactly how
their own work fit in. In 1998, we developed the concept
of spelling out "individual economic values," or IEVs—
short statements that describe how individuals contribute to our profitability. It's a big deal to us to get
these right. Let me give you an example. In her IEV, one
of our consumer relations people specified actions like "I
respond to any customer's call within x hours" and "I am
prompt and courteous in my responses." All true, but not
quite the perspective we need in an IEV. We talked about
it and came up with "I turn every customer I talk to into
a company fan." We want each employee's IEV to communicate—to its owner and to the world—that this is a
person with the power to drive the success of the company. That consumer relations rep is now a person who
can send coupons, make settlements—in short, take
action. A lot of people here have their IEVs printed on
their name badges.

If I'm telling this story clearly, you're starting to see
the culture we were working hard to achieve. We wanted
to create a new world of in-your-face honesty and shared
ownership of results. And that wasn't all. We've developed a list of ten cultural imperatives: honesty, ownership, trust, customer orientation, commitment, fun,
innovation, risk taking, speed and urgency, and teamwork. After we'd agreed on the list, in no particular
order, someone came up with the acronym HOT CC

FIRST—and thank goodness, because we want all our people to be able to recite these values by heart. As a mnemonic, it's not elegant, but I like it that way because it shows that nothing was added or subtracted for the sake of a better catchphrase.

Making Cultural Change a Job: The GDL

If there is one move I credit more than anything else for the success of our cultural makeover, it's our decision to create a role called the growth development leader (GDL). Each GDL (we now have about 70 at Alberto-Culver North America) mentors a dozen or so people, who may or may not be direct reports. We had originally called these people group development leaders because the idea was for them to bring about cultural change at the small group level. We changed the word to "growth" when we realized the role works as a conduit in both directions. It's as important to the growth of the company as it is to the growth of individuals.

GDLs are involved in the careers and lives of the people in their groups, helping to frame IEVs, participating in the performance review process, making sure employees understand and take advantage of all our benefits and human resource policies, and building team spirit. We insist that this be a company that respects family and personal lives; my own priority in life is not a business goal but a personal one: to raise my three children well. GDLs help people throughout the company achieve the right balance for themselves.

I meet with the GDLs every six weeks or so. They are expected to bring forward their people's questions and concerns and, afterward, to share with their groups the topics and solutions we've discussed. At most of the meetings, each brings a group member as a guest. We talk about sales and earnings, new programs, workplace rumors, new products, analyst ratings of our stock—whatever is on their minds and mine. We market the things we're doing well, and we aren't afraid to identify the things we're still doing poorly.

Each year, one of the most important meetings is ded-icated to what we call "macros and irritations." On this occasion—and no one knows in advance which meeting it will be—the GDLs and their guests are split into four subgroups and given just 15 minutes to agree on what they think are the four biggest challenges confronting our business (the macros) and the four most annoying aspects of life at Alberto-Culver (the irritations). Fifteen minutes is pretty much the right amount of time because if an issue doesn't come quickly to mind, it isn't a big deal. We then combine the lists, and I tell the whole group: "Okay, you're the CEO. You have only so many resources, and you can't do it all. Which four deserve our focus?" After the vote, the priorities that rise to the top (and have a chance of being adopted—this is not a pure democracy, and occasionally I scratch one that I know is not right for us) have names assigned to them for follow-up, and we get results. At our last meeting, one of the irritations was not enough laptops for people who are traveling. The CIO and I exchanged a quick glance and conferred over the next break. Several days later, we had a system up and running whereby anyone, on a day's notice, could sign out a laptop with his or her e-mail and requested software programs already installed.

One of the interesting things I've noted over the years is that, in the beginning, the groups weren't coming up with anything I considered a macro. There were lots of irritations back in 1993: our lack of personal days, direct deposit capabilities, and—I'm not kidding here—Post-it notes. But as time went on, the issues got bigger. At this point, our employees are nailing every major business problem we have—such as the need for better recruiting approaches in a full-employment economy. I like to think it's because our people are becoming more strategic thinkers; but it also may be that you have to remove immediate annoyances before people can focus past them. Every year, there's a bigger buzz in the building following this meeting. "What did they make happen this time?" puts pressure on us all to find answers.

Having real power to make change is part of the reason people don't consider it a bother to be a GDL. Quite the contrary: it's an honor. And it's not something that comes automatically with a certain rank; we have GDLs from every rung of the management ladder. The people who serve as GDLs have been handpicked for qualities like empathy, communication skills, positive attitude, and even the ability to let one's hair down and have fun.

Still, being a great GDL isn't everything around here. You can be a really good one and not be promoted if you don't excel at your other work. Our performance review process stands apart from our assessment of people as GDLs. That said, someone who's a superstar as an individual contributor won't get as far—here or, I would expect, anywhere—if he or she can't develop the leadership qualities and people skills that make for a good GDL.

Measure Early, Measure Often

I'm a firm believer that you change what you measure. Once a year, we do an all-employee survey to assess our progress against cultural goals and to gather 360-degree feedback. People are identified by group but are individually anonymous. We include a survey question such as "How much ownership do you personally feel for the company's products?" because when you ask such a question, you're really telling people what you care about. We ask about ethics and team spirit and whether we're having fun yet. We ask about management's success in providing a vision of where the company is going.

The survey for the year 2000 had 180 questions, and 33 focused exclusively on the respondent's GDL. These questions range from the straightforward ("How often does your GDL meet with you?") to the highly subjective ("During the last year, do you feel your GDL has made you feel better, the same, or worse about working for Alberto-Culver?"). Once the results are tabulated, we recognize all the GDLs who scored well in each key category, announce the overall best-scoring GDLs, and reward those folks with company stock.

More important, we sit down and talk with all the GDLs about their results and what's behind them. I personally pore over these surveys. I fret over the people who've shown a downturn; I marvel at those who've outdone themselves. Right now, I'm thinking about the conversation I'll have with one recent hire. She's great at what she does and very much in demand by team leaders around the company, but her GDL scores aren't impressive. My take is, she has the ability but hasn't realized how seriously we take this. Next year, I'd lay money on it, she'll be up toward the front of the pack.

I mentioned that we want people to memorize our list of ten values. It's in our survey ("Do you know our corporate values by heart?"). Do I trust people to answer that one honestly? I do; if people can't answer it when they get to the question, they've since looked it up. This is an open-book test.

Celebrate

I have one last piece of advice. If you want something to grow, pour champagne on it. We've made a huge effort—maybe even an over-the-top effort—to celebrate our successes and, indeed, just about everything we'd like to see happen again. I've already talked about the stock rewards to outstanding GDLs. We also have a program called Business Builders Awards, given to individuals and teams who make a real impact on our growth and profitability, usually by going well beyond their job requirements. A BBA went to someone who spent a month in Mexico helping to upgrade our information systems there. An R&D team working on our TRESemmé product line won recently when their formulation earned a record-breaking score for product performance at the independent testing laboratory we use. And remember those Alberto VO5 shampoo bottles that were earning us only a penny? One team found a way to update the package design and reduce its product cost. A definite business builder.

We also give everyone the chance to vote in our recently launched People's Choice Awards. The 21 categories cover all kinds of things we like to see. Employees vote for the person they'd most like to have on their team; the colleague who best blends commitment to our community with great performance at Alberto-Culver; even, on a lighter note, the person who has the best hair. All of these programs are designed to reinforce central points that we stress at every opportunity: individuals here can make a difference, and companies don't succeed—people do.

Mostly, though, our celebrations aren't awards programs—they're more spontaneous or event-driven. We've thrown a surprise thank-you party to celebrate an exceptional fiscal year, complete with entertainment and 700 pounds of popcorn. On a smaller scale, we note all work anniversaries and personal milestones with "Alberto appropriate" gifts (cheap but tasteful, and not the same for everyone). Many gifts are given from GDLs to their team members and from colleague to colleague just to say thank you—and we have a couple of creative people and a supply room dedicated to the need. The real point is that when someone receives a gift, it sits on a desk for a while, drawing attention. People ask about the occasion, a story is told, and the lesson of what our culture values is reinforced.

Culture Drives Results

With all this discussion of awards and celebration, it may surprise you to hear that we're still considered a tough place to work. We have high expectations of our people, and we don't hesitate to make it clear when they're not living up to them—another aspect of that in-your-face honesty we value. So we talk about having a culture of "caring, not caretaking." We believe in running a fair race. We've removed constraints on people who have the skills and initiative to excel, but we're not carrying poor performers over the finish line.

In a recent acquisition we were not the highest bidder, but the founder chose to go with us because he had a good feeling about our culture.

I'm encouraged to claim we're doing the right things because, certainly, our people are delivering. In my last state of the company address, I reported that our North American sales for 2000 were up 18.2% (corporate sales climbed 13.7%) and our pretax profit was up 25% (corporate net earnings were up 12.6%). These strong growth trends are continuing in FY01 and will produce gains from 1994 through 2001 of 83% in sales and 336% in pretax profit. Over that same period, we've cut employee turnover in half and seen our ability to attract top people from top companies improve. I have the strongest management team right now that's ever been assembled at the company. And great people want to work for great people, so culture and performance tend to become self-perpetuating circles.

Our culture has also had an impact on our success in acquisitions—an important part of our growth story over the past decade. In 1996, when we acquired St. Ives Laboratories, which produces a line of botanically based products, we introduced ourselves to our new colleagues with a version of a state of the company address that made clear how our businesses complemented one another. We offered an honest assessment of St. Ives's strengths and weaknesses and the competitive environment we would now face together. Afterward, many St. Ives employees said that they'd learned more about business on that day than during years of working there. In another recent acquisition, we learned that we had not been the highest bidder but that the founder had chosen to go with us because he had a good feeling about our culture.

> *Passion is probably the single prerequisite to culture change, for those inclined to attempt it. If you're not passionate about it, don't even bother.*

A Passion for Culture

Have we finished the job of changing our culture? Not yet, despite a lot of positive changes. Cultural change, perhaps obviously, is not one change but numerous changes—some big, most little. The majority of them, ultimately, are not mine. I've learned to let our cultural initiatives take on lives of their own. For instance, I've stood back and watched as the head of our sales organization has put his own spin on the GDL teams in his area, urging them to build their emotional intelligence. Meanwhile, our group VP of operations has extended our Business Builders Award to the plant floor, calling the new program "Accolades." There's a lot of ownership of culture around the organization, and it's become a shared passion.

Passion, in fact, is probably the single prerequisite to cultural change, for those inclined to attempt it. If you're not passionate about it, don't even bother. Every decision we make, we now see, is an opportunity to support or to undermine the culture we want. Happily, culture is on a lot of people's minds here now. We've made it an issue and a part of people's jobs, we measure it carefully and celebrate it constantly. As a result, we all enjoy the benefits of greater honesty, ownership, trust, customer orientation, commitment, fun, innovation, risk taking, speed and urgency, and teamwork. It's working today. And we believe if we face tough times at some point in the future, our culture will carry us through. At Alberto-Culver, we have people and we have brands. We care deeply about both.

Alberto-Culver at a Glance

THE ALBERTO-CULVER COMPANY, with 13,000 employees worldwide, is a $2.25 billion manufacturer and marketer of personal care, specialty grocery, and household products. Its Sally Beauty Company, with more the 2,000 stores in the United States, United Kingdom, Canada, Germany, and Japan, is the world's largest distributor of professional salon products.

Its consumer packaged goods are sold in more than 130 countries. The portfolio includes global brands such as the company's flagship Alberto VO5 hair care line and St. Ives skin care, facial, and hair care products, as well as a number of other well-known brands: Consort,

A Culture on the Move:
Alberto-Culver North America

The cultural changes within Alberto-Culver North America since 1993 have underpinned corporate growth.

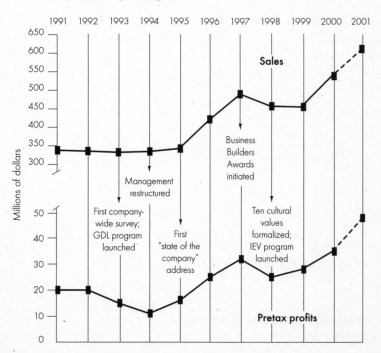

FDS, Just for Me, Molly McButter, Motions, Mrs. Dash, Static Guard, and TRESemmé in the United States, and, internationally, strong portfolios of regional personal care and household brands ranging from Salveqvik bandages and Samarin antacid to the Indola professional hair care line.

In consumer products, Alberto-Culver's competitors include Procter & Gamble and Unilever, and its customers include the largest and most demanding retailers in the world. Despite that, in a market with relatively flat growth rates, the company has reported nine consecutive years of record sales and earnings, most at double-digit rates. Its packaged goods businesses, after plateauing in the early1990s, have shown accelerating sales and profit growth rates throughout the last half of the decade.

Originally published in June 2001
Reprint R0106B

Conquering a Culture of Indecision

RAM CHARAN

Executive Summary

THE SINGLE GREATEST CAUSE of corporate underperformance is the failure to execute. Author Ram Charan, drawing on a quarter century of observing organizational behavior, perceives that such failures of execution share a family resemblance: a misfire in the personal interactions that are supposed to produce results.

Faulty interactions rarely occur in isolation, Charan says. Far more often, they're typical of the way large and small decisions are made or not made throughout the organization. The inability to take decisive action is rooted in a company's culture.

But, Charan notes, leaders create a culture of indecisiveness, and leaders can break it. Breaking it requires them to take three actions. First, they must engender intellectual honesty in the connections between people. Second, they must see to it that the organization's "social operating mechanisms"–the meetings, reviews, and other situations through which people in the corporation do business–have honest dialogue at their cores. And third, leaders must ensure that feedback and follow-through are used to reward high achievers, coach those who are struggling, and discourage those whose behavior are blocking the organization's progress.

By taking these three approaches and using every encounter as an opportunity to model open and honest dialogue, a leader can set the tone for an organization, moving it from paralysis to action.

DOES THIS SOUND FAMILIAR? You're sitting in the quarterly business review as a colleague plows through a two-inch-thick proposal for a big investment in a new product. When he finishes, the room falls quiet. People look left, right, or down, waiting for someone else to open the discussion. No one wants to comment—at least not until the boss shows which way he's leaning.

Finally, the CEO breaks the loud silence. He asks a few mildly skeptical questions to show he's done his due diligence. But it's clear that he has made up his mind to back the project. Before long, the other meeting attendees are chiming in dutifully, careful to keep their comments positive. Judging from the remarks, it appears that everyone in the room supports the project.

But appearances can be deceiving. The head of a related division worries that the new product will take resources away from his operation. The vice president of manufacturing thinks that the first-year sales forecasts are wildly optimistic and will leave him with a warehouse full of unsold goods. Others in the room are lukewarm because they don't see how they stand to gain from the project. But they keep their reservations to themselves, and the meeting breaks up inconclusively. Over the next few months, the project is slowly strangled to death in a series of strategy, budget, and operational reviews. It's not clear who's responsible for the killing, but it's plain that the true sentiment in the room was the opposite of the apparent consensus.

In my career as an adviser to large organizations and their leaders, I have witnessed many occasions even at the highest levels when silent lies and a lack of closure lead to false decisions. They are "false" because they eventually get undone by unspoken factors and inaction. And after a quarter century of firsthand observations, I have concluded that these instances of indecision share a family resemblance—a misfire in the personal interactions that are supposed to produce results. The people charged with reaching a decision and acting on it fail to connect and engage with one another. Intimidated by the group dynamics of hierarchy and constrained by formality and lack of trust, they speak their lines woodenly and without conviction. Lacking emotional commitment, the people who must carry out the plan don't act decisively.

These faulty interactions rarely occur in isolation. Far more often, they're typical of the way large and small decisions are made—or not made—throughout a company. The inability to take decisive action is rooted in the corporate culture and seems to employees to be impervious to change.

The key word here is "seems," because, in fact, leaders create a culture of indecisiveness, and leaders can break it. The primary instrument at their disposal is the human interactions—the dialogues—through which assumptions are challenged or go unchallenged, information is shared or not shared, disagreements are brought to the surface or papered over. Dialogue is the basic unit of work in an organization. The quality of the dialogue determines how people gather and process information, how they make decisions, and how they feel about one another and about the outcome of these decisions. Dialogue can lead to new ideas and speed as a competitive advantage. It is the single-most important factor underlying the productivity and growth of the knowledge worker. Indeed, the tone and content of dialogue shapes people's behaviors and beliefs—that is, the corporate culture—faster and more permanently than any reward system, structural change, or vision statement I've seen.

Breaking a culture of indecision requires a leader who can engender intellectual honesty and trust in the connections between people. By using each encounter with his or her employees as an opportunity to model open, honest, and decisive dialogue, the leader sets the tone for the entire organization.

But setting the tone is only the first step. To transform a culture of indecision, leaders must also see to it that the organization's "social operating mechanisms"—that is, the executive committee meetings, budget and strategy reviews, and other situations through which the people of a corporation do business—have honest dialogue at their center. These mechanisms set the stage. Tightly linked and consistently practiced, they establish clear lines of accountability for reaching decisions and executing them.

Follow-through and feedback are the final steps in creating a decisive culture. Successful leaders use follow-through and honest feedback to reward high achievers, coach those who are struggling, and redirect the behaviors of those blocking the organization's progress.

In sum, leaders can create a culture of decisive behavior through attention to their own dialogue, the careful design of social operating mechanisms, and appropriate follow-through and feedback.

It All Begins with Dialogue

Studies of successful companies often focus on their products, business models, or operational strengths: Microsoft's world-conquering Windows operating system, Dell's mass customization, Wal-Mart's logistical prowess. Yet products and operational strengths aren't what really set the most successful organizations apart— they can all be rented or imitated. What can't be easily duplicated are the decisive dialogues and robust operating mechanisms and their links to feedback and follow-through. These factors constitute an organization's most enduring competitive advantage, and they are heavily dependent on the character of dialogue that a leader exhibits and thereby influences throughout the organization.

Decisive dialogue is easier to recognize than to define. It encourages incisiveness and creativity and brings coherence to seemingly fragmented and unrelated ideas. It allows tensions to surface and then resolves them by fully airing every relevant viewpoint. Because such dialogue is a process of intellectual inquiry rather than of advocacy, a search for truth rather than a contest, people feel emotionally committed to the outcome. The outcome seems "right" because people have helped shape it. They are energized and ready to act.

Not long ago, I observed the power of a leader's dialogue to shape a company's culture. The setting was the headquarters of a major U.S. multinational. The head of one of the company's largest business units was making a strategy presentation to the CEO and a few of his senior lieutenants. Sounding confident, almost cocky, the unit head laid out his strategy for taking his division from number three in Europe to number one. It was an ambitious plan that hinged on making rapid, sizable market-share gains in Germany, where the company's main competitor was locally based and four times his division's size. The CEO commended his unit head for the inspiring and visionary presentation, then initiated a dialogue to test whether the plan was realistic. "Just how are you going to make these gains?" he wondered aloud. "What other alternatives have you considered? What customers do you plan to acquire?" The unit manager hadn't thought that far ahead. "How have you defined the customers' needs in new and unique ways? How many salespeople do you have?" the CEO asked.

"Ten," answered the unit head.

"How many does your main competitor have?"

"Two hundred," came the sheepish reply.

The boss continued to press: "Who runs Germany for us? Wasn't he in another division up until about three months ago?"

Had the exchange stopped there, the CEO would have only humiliated and discouraged this unit head and sent a message to others in attendance that the risks of thinking big were unacceptably high. But the CEO wasn't interested in killing the strategy and demoralizing the business unit team. Coaching through questioning, he wanted to inject some realism into the dialogue. Speaking bluntly, but not angrily or unkindly, he told the unit manager that he would need more than bravado to take on a formidable German competitor on its home turf. Instead of making a frontal assault, the CEO suggested, why not look for the competition's weak spots and win on speed of execution? Where are the gaps in your competitor's product line? Can you innovate something that can fill those gaps? What customers are the most likely buyers of such a product? Why not zero in on them? Instead of aiming for overall market-share gains, try resegmenting the market. Suddenly, what had appeared to be a dead end opened into new insights, and by the end of the meeting, it was decided that the manager would rethink the strategy and return in 90 days with a more realistic alternative. A key player whose strategy proposal had been flatly rejected left the room feeling energized, challenged, and more sharply focused on the task at hand.

Think about what happened here. Although it might not have been obvious at first, the CEO was not trying to assert his authority or diminish the executive. He simply wanted to ensure that the competitive realities were not glossed over and to coach those in attendance on both business acumen and organizational capability as well as on the fine art of asking the right questions. He was challenging the proposed strategy not for personal reasons but for business reasons.

The dialogue affected people's attitudes and behavior in subtle and not so subtle ways: they walked away knowing that they should look for opportunities in unconventional ways and be prepared to answer the inevitable tough questions. They also knew that the CEO was on their side. They became more convinced that growth was possible and that action was necessary. And something else happened: they began to adopt the CEO's tone in subsequent meetings. When, for example, the head of the German unit met with his senior staff to brief them on the new approach to the German market, the questions he fired at his sales chief and product development head were pointed, precise, and aimed directly at putting the new strategy into action. He had picked up on his boss's style of relating to others as well as his way of eliciting, sifting, and analyzing information. The entire unit grew more determined and energized.

The chief executive didn't leave the matter there, though. He followed up with a one-page, handwritten letter to the unit head stating the essence of the dialogue and the actions to be executed. And in 90 days, they met again to discuss the revised strategy. (For more on fostering decisive dialogue, see "Dialogue Killers" at the end of this article.)

How Dialogue Becomes Action

The setting in which dialogue occurs is as important as the dialogue itself. The social operating mechanisms of decisive corporate cultures feature behaviors marked by four characteristics: openness, candor, informality, and closure. Openness means that the outcome is not predetermined. There's an honest search for alternatives and new discoveries. Questions like "What are we missing?" draw people in and signal the leader's willingness to hear all sides. Leaders create an atmosphere of safety that permits spirited discussion, group learning, and trust.

Candor is slightly different. It's a willingness to speak the unspeakable, to expose unfulfilled commitments, to air the conflicts that undermine apparent consensus. Candor means that people express their real opinions, not what they think team players are supposed to say. Candor helps wipe out the silent lies and pocket vetoes that occur when people agree to things they have no intention of acting on. It prevents the kind of unnecessary rework and revisiting of decisions that saps productivity.

Formality suppresses candor; informality encourages it. When presentations and comments are stiff and prepackaged, they signal that the whole meeting has been carefully scripted and orchestrated. Informality has the opposite effect. It reduces defensiveness. People feel more comfortable asking questions and reacting honestly, and the spontaneity is energizing.

If informality loosens the atmosphere, closure imposes discipline. Closure means that at the end of the meeting, people know exactly what they are expected to do. Closure produces decisiveness by assigning accountability and deadlines to people in an open forum. It tests a leader's inner strength and intellectual resources. Lack of closure, coupled with a lack of sanctions, is the primary reason for a culture of indecision.

A robust social operating mechanism consistently includes these four characteristics. Such a mechanism has the right people participating in it, and it occurs with the right frequency.

When Dick Brown arrived at Electronic Data Systems (EDS) in early 1999, he resolved to create a culture that did more than pay lip service to the ideals of collaboration, openness, and decisiveness. He had a big job ahead of him. EDS was known for its bright, aggressive people, but employees had a reputation for competing against one another at least as often as they pulled together. The organization was marked by a culture of lone heroes. Individual operating units had little

It's not enough for a manager to say she's assessing, reviewing, or analyzing a problem. Those aren't the words of someone who is acting.

or no incentive for sharing information or cooperating with one another to win business. There were few sanctions for "lone" behaviors and for failure to meet performance goals. And indecision was rife. As one company veteran puts it, "Meetings, meetings, and more meetings. People couldn't make decisions, wouldn't make decisions. They didn't have to. No accountability." EDS was losing business. Revenue was flat, earnings were on the decline, and the price of the company's stock was down sharply.

A central tenet of Brown's management philosophy is that "leaders get the behavior they tolerate." Shortly after he arrived at EDS, he installed six social operating mechanisms within one year that signaled he would not put up with the old culture of rampant individualism and information hoarding. One mechanism was the "performance call," as it is known around the company. Once a month, the top 100 or so EDS executives worldwide take part in a conference call where the past month's numbers and critical activities are reviewed in detail. Transparency and simultaneous information are the rules; information hoarding is no longer possible. Everyone knows who is on target for the year, who is ahead of projections, and who is behind. Those who are behind must explain the shortfall—and how they plan to get back on track. It's not enough for a manager to say she's assessing, reviewing, or analyzing a problem. Those aren't the words of someone who is acting, Brown says. Those are the words of someone getting ready to act. To use them in front of Brown is to invite two questions in response: When you've finished your analysis, what are you going to do? And how soon are you going to do it? The only way that Brown's people can answer those questions satisfactorily is to make a decision and execute it.

The performance calls are also a mechanism for airing and resolving the conflicts inevitable in a large organization, particularly when it comes to cross-selling in order to accelerate revenue growth. Two units may be pursuing the same customer, for example, or a customer serviced by one unit may be acquired by a customer serviced by another. Which unit should lead the pursuit? Which unit should service the merged entity? It's vitally important to resolve these questions. Letting them fester doesn't just drain emotional energy, it shrinks the organization's capacity to act decisively. Lack of speed becomes a competitive disadvantage.

Brown encourages people to bring these conflicts to the surface, both because he views them as a sign of organizational health and because they provide an opportunity to demonstrate the style of dialogue he advocates. He tries to create a safe environment for disagreement by reminding employees that the conflict isn't personal. Conflict in any global organization is built in. And, Brown believes, it's essential if everyone is going to think in terms of the entire organization, not just one little corner of it. Instead of seeking the solution favorable to their unit, they'll look for the solution that's best for EDS and its shareholders. It sounds simple, even obvious. But in an organization once characterized by lone heroes and self-interest, highly visible exercises in conflict resolution remind people to align their interests with the company as a whole. It's not enough to state the message once and assume it will sink in. Behavior is changed through repetition. Stressing the message over and over in social operating mechanisms like the monthly performance calls—and rewarding or sanctioning people based on their adherence to it—is one of Brown's most powerful tools for producing the behavioral changes that usher in genuine cultural change.

Of course, no leader can or should attend every meeting, resolve every conflict, or make every decision. But by designing social operating mechanisms that promote free-flowing yet productive dialogue, leaders strongly influence how others perform these tasks. Indeed, it is through these mechanisms that the work of shaping a decisive culture gets done.

Another corporation that employs social operating mechanisms to create a decisive culture is multinational pharmaceutical giant Pharmacia. The company's approach illustrates a point I stress repeatedly to my clients: structure divides; social operating mechanisms integrate. I hasten to add that structure is essential. If an organization didn't divide tasks, functions, and responsibilities, it would never get anything done. But social operating mechanisms are required to direct the various activities contained within a structure toward an objective. Well-designed mechanisms perform this integrating function. But no matter how well designed, the mechanisms also need decisive dialogue to work properly.

Two years after its 1995 merger with Upjohn, Pharmacia's CEO Fred Hassan set out to create an entirely new culture for the combined entity. The organization he envisioned would be collaborative, customer focused, and speedy. It would meld the disparate talents of a global enterprise to develop market-leading drugs—and do so faster than the competition. The primary mechanism for fostering collaboration: leaders from several units and functions would engage in frequent, constructive dialogue.

The company's race to develop a new generation of antibiotics to treat drug-resistant infections afforded

Pharmacia's management an opportunity to test the success of its culture-building efforts. Dr. Göran Endo, the chief of research and development, and Carrie Cox, the head of global business management, jointly created a social operating mechanism comprising some of the company's leading scientists, clinicians, and marketers. Just getting the three functions together regularly was a bold step. Typically, drug development proceeds by a series of hand-offs. One group of scientists does the basic work of drug discovery, then hands off its results to a second group, which steers the drug through a year or more of clinical trials. If and when it receives the Food and Drug Administration's stamp of approval, it's handed off to the marketing people, who devise a marketing plan. Only then is the drug handed off to the sales department, which pitches it to doctors and hospitals. By supplanting this daisy-chain approach with one that made scientists, clinicians, and marketers jointly responsible for the entire flow of development and marketing, the two leaders aimed to develop a drug that better met the needs of patients, had higher revenue potential, and gained speed as a competitive advantage. And they wanted to create a template for future collaborative efforts.

The company's reward system reinforced this collaborative model by explicitly linking compensation to the actions of the group. Every member's compensation would be based on the time to bring the drug to market, the time for the drug to reach peak profitable share, and total sales. The system gave group members a strong incentive to talk openly with one another and to share information freely. But the creative spark was missing. The first few times the drug development group met, it focused almost exclusively on their differences, which

were considerable. Without trafficking in clichés, it is
safe to say that scientists, clinicians, and marketers tend
to have different ways of speaking, thinking, and relating.
And each tended to defend what it viewed as its interests
rather than the interests of shareholders and customers.
It was at this point that Endo and Cox took charge of the
dialogue, reminding the group that it was important to
play well with others but, even more important, to produce a drug that met patients' needs and to beat the
competition.

Acting together, the two leaders channeled conversation into productive dialogue focused on a common task.
They shared what they knew about developing and marketing pharmaceuticals and demonstrated how scientists could learn to think a little like marketers, and marketers a little like scientists. They tackled the emotional
challenge of resolving conflicts in the open in order to
demonstrate how to disagree, sometimes strongly, without animosity and without losing sight of their common
purpose.

Indeed, consider how one dialogue helped the group
make a decision that turned a promising drug into a success story. To simplify the research and testing process,
the group's scientists had begun to search for an
antibiotic that would be effective against a limited
number of infections and would be used only as
"salvage therapy" in acute cases, when conventional
antibiotic therapies had failed. But intensive dialogue with the marketers yielded
the information that doctors were receptive to a drug

*Few mechanisms encourage
directness more effectively
than performance and
compensation reviews,
especially if they are
explicitly linked to social
operating mechanisms.*

that would work against a wide spectrum of infections. They wanted a drug that could treat acute infections completely by starting treatment earlier in the course of the disease, either in large doses through an intravenous drip or in smaller doses with a pill. The scientists shifted their focus, and the result was Zyvox, one of the major pharmaceutical success stories of recent years. It has become the poster drug in Pharmacia's campaign for a culture characterized by cross-functional collaboration and speedy execution. Through dialogue, the group created a product that neither the scientists, clinicians, nor marketers acting by themselves could have envisioned or executed. And the mechanism that created this open dialogue is now standard practice at Pharmacia.

Follow-Through and Feedback

Follow-through is in the DNA of decisive cultures and takes place either in person, on the telephone, or in the routine conduct of a social operating mechanism. Lack of follow-through destroys the discipline of execution and encourages indecision.

A culture of indecision changes when groups of people are compelled to always be direct. And few mechanisms encourage directness more effectively than performance and compensation reviews, especially if they are explicitly linked to social operating mechanisms. Yet all too often, the performance review process is as ritualized and empty as the business meeting I described at the beginning of this article. Both the employee and his manager want to get the thing over with as quickly as possible. Check the appropriate box, keep up the good work, here's your raise, and let's be sure to do this again next year. Sorry—gotta run. There's no genuine conversation,

no feedback, and worst of all, no chance for the employee
to learn the sometimes painful truths that will help her
grow and develop. Great compensation systems die for
lack of candid dialogue and leaders' emotional fortitude.

At EDS, Dick Brown has devised an evaluation and
review process that virtually forces managers to engage
in candid dialogue with their subordinates. Everyone at
the company is ranked in quintiles and rewarded according to how well they perform compared with their peers.
It has proved to be one of the most controversial features
of Dick Brown's leadership—some employees view it as a
Darwinian means of dividing winners from losers and
pitting colleagues against one another.

That isn't the objective of the ranking system, Brown
insists. He views the ranking process as the most effective way to reward the company's best performers and
show laggards where
they need to improve.
But the system needs the
right sort of dialogue to
make it work as intended
and serve its purpose of
growing the talent pool.

*By failing to provide honest
feedback, leaders cheat their
people by depriving them
of the information they need
to improve.*

Leaders must give honest feedback to their direct
reports, especially to those who find themselves at the
bottom of the rankings.

Brown recalls one encounter he had shortly after the
first set of rankings was issued. An employee who had
considered himself one of EDS's best performers was
shocked to find himself closer to the bottom of the roster
than the top. "How could this be?" the employee asked. "I
performed as well this year as I did last year, and last
year my boss gave me a stellar review." Brown replied
that he could think of two possible explanations. The

first was that the employee wasn't as good at his job as he thought he was. The second possibility was that even if the employee was doing as good a job as he did the previous year, his peers were doing better. "If you're staying the same," Brown concluded, "you're falling behind."

That exchange revealed the possibility—the likelihood, even—that the employee's immediate superior had given him a less-than-honest review the year before rather than tackle the unpleasant task of telling him where he was coming up short. Brown understands why a manager might be tempted to duck such a painful conversation. Delivering negative feedback tests the strength of a leader. But critical feedback is part of what Brown calls "the heavy lifting of leadership." Avoiding it, he says, "sentences the organization to mediocrity." What's more, by failing to provide honest feedback, leaders cheat their people by depriving them of the information they need to improve.

Feedback should be many things—candid; constructive; relentlessly focused on behavioral performance, accountability, and execution. One thing it shouldn't be is surprising. "A leader should be constructing his appraisal all year long," Brown says, "and giving his appraisal all year long. You have 20, 30, 60 opportunities a year to share your observations. Don't let those opportunities pass. If, at the end of the year, someone is truly surprised by what you have to say, that's a failure of leadership."

Ultimately, changing a culture of indecision is a matter of leadership. It's a matter of asking hard questions: How robust and effective are our social operating mechanisms? How well are they linked? Do they have the right people and the right frequency? Do they have a rhythm and operate consistently? Is follow-through built in? Are rewards and sanctions linked to the outcomes of the decisive dialogue? Most important, how productive is the dialogue within these mechanisms? Is our dialogue marked by openness, candor, informality, and closure?

Transforming a culture of indecision is an enormous and demanding task. It takes all the listening skills, business acumen, and operational experience that a corporate leader can summon. But just as important, the job demands emotional fortitude, follow-through, and inner strength. Asking the right questions, identifying and resolving conflicts, providing candid, constructive feedback, and differentiating people with sanctions and rewards is never easy. Frequently, it's downright unpleasant. No wonder many senior executives avoid the task. In the short term, they spare themselves considerable emotional wear and tear. But their evasion sets the tone for an organization that can't share intelligence, make decisions, or face conflicts, much less resolve them. Those who evade miss the very point of effective leadership. Leaders with the strength to insist on honest dialogue and follow-through will be rewarded not only with a decisive organization but also with a workforce that is energized, empowered, and engaged.

Dialogue Killers

IS THE DIALOGUE IN YOUR MEETINGS an energy drain? If it doesn't energize people and focus their work, watch for the following:

Dangling Dialogue

Symptom: Confusion prevails. The meeting ends without a clear next step. People create their own self-serving interpretations of the meeting, and no one can be held accountable later when goals aren't met.

Remedy: Give the meeting closure by ensuring that everyone knows who will do what, by when. Do it in writing if necessary, and be specific.

Information Clogs

Symptom: Failure to get all the relevant information into the open. An important fact or opinion comes to light after a decision has been reached, which reopens the decision. This pattern happens repeatedly.

Remedy: Ensure that the right people are in attendance in the first place. When missing information is discovered, disseminate it immediately. Make the expectation for openness and candor explicit by asking, "What's missing?" Use coaching and sanctions to correct information hoarding.

Piecemeal Perspectives

Symptom: People stick to narrow views and self-interests and fail to acknowledge that others have valid interests.

Remedy: Draw people out until you're sure all sides of the issue have been represented. Restate the common purpose repeatedly to keep everyone focused on the big picture. Generate alternatives. Use coaching to show people how their work contributes to the overall mission of the enterprise.

Free for All

Symptom: By failing to direct the flow of the discussion, the leader allows negative behaviors to flourish. "Extortionists" hold the whole group for ransom until others see it their way; "sidetrackers" go off on tangents, recount history by saying "When I did this ten years ago...," or delve into unnecessary detail; "silent liars" do not express

their true opinions, or they agree to things they have no
intention of doing; and "dividers" create breaches within
the group by seeking support for their viewpoint outside
the social operating mechanism or have parallel discus-
sions during the meeting.

Remedy: The leader must exercise inner strength by
repeatedly signaling which behaviors are acceptable
and by sanctioning those who persist in negative
behavior. If less severe sanctions fail, the leader must
be willing to remove the offending player from the
group.

GE's Secret Weapon

KNOWN FOR ITS STATE-OF-THE-ART management
practices, General Electric has forged a system of ten
tightly linked social operating mechanisms. Vital to GE's
success, these mechanisms set goals and priorities for the
whole company as well as for its individual business units
and track each unit's progress toward those goals. CEO
Jack Welch also uses the system to evaluate senior managers within each unit and reward or sanction them
according to their performance.

Three of the most widely imitated of these mechanisms are the Corporate Executive Council (CEC), which
meets four times a year; the annual leadership and organizational reviews, known as Session C; and the annual
strategy reviews, known as S-1 and S-2. Most large
organizations have similar mechanisms. GE's, however,
are notable for their intensity and duration; tight links to
one another; follow-through; and uninhibited candor, closure, and decisiveness.

At the CEC, the company's senior leaders gather for two-and-a-half days of intensive collaboration and information exchange. As these leaders share best practices, assess the external business environment, and identify the company's most promising opportunities and most pressing problems, Welch has a chance to coach managers and observe their styles of working, thinking, and collaborating. Among the ten initiatives to emerge from these meetings in the past 14 years are GE's six sigma quality-improvement drive and its companywide e-commerce effort. These sessions aren't for the fainthearted—at times, the debates can resemble verbal combat. But by the time the CEC breaks up, everyone in attendance knows both what the corporate priorities are and what's expected of him or her.

At Session C meetings, Welch and GE's senior vice president for human resources, Bill Conaty, meet with the head of each business unit as well as his or her top HR executive to discuss leadership and organizational issues. In these intense 12- to 14-hour sessions, the attendees review the unit's prospective talent pool and its organizational priorities. Who needs to be promoted, rewarded, and developed? How? Who isn't making the grade? Candor is mandatory, and so is execution. The dialogue goes back and forth and links with the strategy of the business unit. Welch follows up each session with a handwritten note reviewing the substance of the dialogue and action items. Through this mechanism, picking and evaluating people has become a core competence at GE. No wonder GE is known as "CEO University."

The unit head's progress in implementing that action plan is among the items on the agenda at the S-1 meeting, held about two months after Session C. Welch, his chief financial officer, and members of the office of the

CEO meet individually with each unit head and his or her team to discuss strategy for the next three years. The strategy, which must incorporate the companywide themes and initiatives that emerged from the CEC meetings, is subjected to intensive scrutiny and reality testing by Welch and the senior staff. The dialogue in the sessions is informal, open, decisive, and full of valuable coaching from Welch on both business and human resources issues. As in Session C, the dialogue about strategy links with people and organizational issues. Again, Welch follows up with a handwritten note in which he sets out what he expects of the unit head as a result of the dialogue.

S-2 meetings, normally held in November, follow a similar agenda to the S-1 meeting, except that they are focused on a shorter time horizon, usually 12 to 15 months. Here, operational priorities and resource allocations are linked.

Taken together, the meetings link feedback, decision making, and assessment of the organization's capabilities and key people. The mechanism explicitly ties the goals and performance of each unit to the overall strategy of the corporation and places a premium on the development of the next generation of leaders. The process is unrelenting in its demand for managerial accountability. At the same time, Welch takes the opportunity to engage in follow-through and feedback that is candid, on point, and focused on decisiveness and execution. This operating system may be GE's most enduring competitive advantage.

Originally published in April 2001
Reprint R0104D

About the Contributors

CAROL LAVIN BERNICK's twenty-eight year career with the Alberto-Culver Company has been focused on her strengths in marketing, new product development, and strategic management. Today she holds dual positions as president of Alberto-Culver North America and vice-chair of the corporation. As president she oversees manufacturing, distribution, research, new product development, and sales and marketing for four North American business units. These include the company's beauty and personal care brands such as Alberto VO5, St. Ives, and TRESemmé; specialty brands, including products which she originated—Mrs. Dash, Molly McButter, and Static Guard; Pro-Line International—the second largest manufacturer of hair care products for people of color in the world; and a custom packaging operation. In her role as vice-chair, she directs companywide initiatives in the areas of strategic planning, human resources, crisis management, community involvement, and corporate culture. She has been cited for her accomplishments in publications such as *Fortune, Working Woman,* and *Women of the Next Millennium.* She is active in the community in a wide variety of groups focused on health care, education, and the advancement of women.

RAM CHARAN is an adviser to CEOs and top managers of some of the world's largest companies. Among his clients are GE, DuPont, Home Depot, and EDS. Mr. Charan is the author or coauthor of ten books, including *What the CEO Wants You to Know*, *The Leadership Pipeline*, *Every Business Is a Growth Business*, and *Boards at Work*. He also has written books tailored for companies such as Ford, EDS, and Gateway. His most recent book, *Execution: The Discipline of Getting Things Done*, coauthored by Larry Bossidy, will be published in May 2002. Charan was elected a fellow of the National Academy of Human Resources and was named by *Business Week* as the number two resource for in-house executive education. He is on the editorial review board of Human Resource Planning and served on the Blue Ribbon Commission on Corporate Governance. Mr. Charan is based in Dallas, Texas.

KATHERINE M. HUDSON has been president and Chief Executive Officer of Brady Corporation, an international manufacturer of identification and material solution products, since January 1994. Prior to her appointment at Brady, Ms. Hudson was corporate vice president and general manager of Eastman Kodak's Professional Printing and Publishing Imaging Division. Her twenty-four years at Kodak included positions in finance, communication and public affairs, information systems, and the management of the instant photography, printing, and publishing business units. She is a director of CNH Global, N.V. and Charming Shoppes, Inc., and also serves on the Alverno College Board of Trustees, the Medical College of Wisconsin Board of Trustees, the National Technology Advisory Board of the Milwaukee Public School System, the Wisconsin United for Health Foundation, and the Wisconsin Manufacturer and Commerce Board. She has received numerous awards, including the Sacajawea Award presented by Professional Dimensions, Inc., Wisconsin Business Leader of the Year presented by the Harvard Business School Alumni Association and the Milwaukee *Journal Sentinel*, and the Breaking the Glass Ceiling Award from the Women Executives in State Government organization. She was listed as one of the 100 Strategists to Watch in the *Journal of Business Strategy*, recognized as one of America's Most Powerful Women Managers by *Executive Female*, and named as one of the twelve most influential CIOs of the decade by *CIO*. In 1993 she was listed by *Industry Week* as a national leader in research and development. In 1990 she was recognized as *Information Week*'s Information Officer of the Year for her innovative use of strategic alliances in information technology.

ROBERT KEGAN is the William and Miriam Meehan Professor of Adult Learning and Professional Development at the Harvard University Graduate School of Education. He is the coauthor of *How the Way We Talk Can Change the Way We Work: Seven Languages for Transformation* and cofounder of Minds at Work, a consulting firm specializing in issues of mental complexity in organizational life [www.mindsatwork.com].

LISA LASKOW LAHEY is the research director of the Change Leadership Group at the Harvard University Graduate School of Education. She is the coauthor of *How the Way We Talk Can Change the Way We Work: Seven Languages for Transformation* and cofounder of Minds at Work, a consulting firm specializing in issues of mental complexity in organizational life [www.mindsatwork.com].

PAUL F. LEVY was appointed president and Chief Executive Officer of the Beth Israel Deaconess Medical Center in Boston in January 2002. The BIDMC is one of the nation's preeminent academic health centers, providing state-of-the-art clinical care research and teaching in affiliation with Harvard Medical School. Previously, Mr. Levy was the executive dean for administration at Harvard Medical School, where he was responsible for administrative, budgetary, and facility issues, as well as community and governmental relations. He was also involved in coordinating collaborative ventures between HMS and its affiliated hospitals. Before joining Harvard Medical School, Paul Levy was adjunct professor of environmental policy at MIT, where he taught infrastructure planning and development and environmental policy for seven years. He has also maintained an independent consulting practice, providing strategic, negotiation, and regulatory advice to firms in the energy, water, and telecommunications arenas. Mr. Levy has served as executive director of the Massachusetts Water Resources Authority, chairman of the Massachusetts department of Public Utilities, and director of the Arkansas Department of Energy. At the MWRA, he had primary responsibility for the "Boston Harbor Cleanup," one of the largest pollution control projects in the world. He currently serves on the Board of Directors for the Harvard Clinical Research Institute and Water Solutions Group, LLC.

DEBRA E. MEYERSON is author of *Tempered Radicals: How People Use Difference to Inspire Change at Work*. She is visiting professor of organizational behavior at Stanford University's Graduate School of Business and at the Center for Work, Technology, and Organization within Stanford's School of Engineering. She is also affiliated faculty at the Center for Gender in Organizations at the Simmons Graduate School of Management and at Stanford's Center for Social Innovation and Center for Comparative Study of Race and Ethnicity. Professor Meyerson has published more than thirty articles and chapters in scholarly and applied publications and has given seminars for companies and non-profit organizations throughout the world. She was selected as one of the Bay Area's "seventy-five most influential women in business" by the *San Francisco Business Times* and has been the recipient of a number of awards and grants, most recently from the Ford Foundation.

BILL MUNCK began his carrer with Marriott over twenty-nine years ago after attending the University of Massachusetts Amherst. He's been a general manager at four Marriott Hotels, including the Copley Marriot—a 1,200-room convention hotel located in Boston's Back Bay. In his current role as market vice president, he is responsible for overseeing fourteen full-service hotels located throughout New England. Along with numerous other affiliates, he serves as vice-chair for Boston's Convention & Visitor's Bureau.

DONALD N. SULL is an assistant professor of business administration in the entrepreneurial management area of the Harvard Business School. Professor Sull's research explores how strong commitments lock firms into the status quo and also provide a tool for managers to successfully overcome corporate inertia. His book on overcoming inertia is scheduled for publication in January 2003. Prior to joining the Harvard faculty, Sull served as an assistant professor at the London Business School where he won the school's Best Teacher Award.

Index

procedures. *See* management
processes
Procter & Gamble, 129, 142

quality, and face time, 26–27,
33–34

radical change. *See* tempered
radicalism
relationships
active inertia and, 96–98
as obstacle to effectiveness,
41–42, 53–54
Renault, 100
resistance to change, 37–58.
See also competing
commitments
diagnosis of, 42–43, 48–49
examples of competing
commitments and, 40–42
groups and, 56–58
managers and, 53–54
notion of competing com-
mitments and, 38–39
process for overcoming,
39–40
response to change. *See* active
inertia
results, and cultural change,
32–34, 126, 138–139
revolution, and corporate
change, 99–103
reward system
celebration of successes and,
126, 129–130, 136,
137–138

decisive cultures and,
153–154, 155–156
fun culture and, 115–116
risk-taking and, 25–26
teams and, 20
Ricoh, 93
risk taking
as cultural imperative, 132
fun culture and, 111, 112
reward system and, 25–26
RJR Nabisco, 102
Robertson, Pat, 90
rough times, 114–115
Royal Dutch/Shell, 99

S-1 meetings at GE, 162,
163–164
S-2 meetings at GE, 162, 164
St. Ives Laboratories, 139, 141
Sally Beauty Company
(Alberto-Culver brand),
127, 131–132, 141
Samsung, 100
Schrempp, Jürgen, 105
Scully, Maureen, 78
self-interested perspectives,
161
senior management. *See
also* leadership; Nut
Island effect; tempered
radicalism
example setting and, 31,
116–117, 146, 148–150
immunity to change and,
53–54
quiet change and, 60–62